When Songs are Forbidden

When Songs Are Forbidden

The True Story of a
Children's Choir
in Romania

Genovieva Sfatcu Beattie
with Stephen Beattie

VMI PUBLISHERS • SISTERS, OREGON

Published by
VMI Publishers
Sisters, Oregon
www.vmipublishers.com

All Scripture references are taken from the *Holy Bible, New International Version.* Copyright © 1973, 1978, 1984 International Bible Society. Used by permission of Zondervan Bible Publishers.

ISBN: 978-1-933204-82-6
ISBN: 1-933204-82-6

Library of Congress: 2008943813

Printed in the USA

Cover by Juanita Dix

Note: Some of the names in this book have been changed.

CONTENTS

ACKNOWLEDGMENTS

As a correspondence student with the Institute of Children's Literature and Long Ridge Writers Group, West Redding, Connecticut, between 1994 and 1999, I should like to thank my wonderful instructors, Jean Soule, Ethel Paquin, Venita Helton, Patricia Pfitsch, and Kristi Holl, who taught me to write and helped me to break into print.

My special thanks go also to my husband, Stephen, who encouraged me to go on as I recalled the sad experiences from my life. He made many valuable suggestions and helped me at every stage, from typing the first draft to preparing the final manuscript for the publisher.

Genovieva Sfatcu Beattie

PART ONE

Chapter One

A Word from the Lord

"You are expelled from this university," announced the secretary. "You are not allowed to enter any other institute of higher education—because of your Christian activities."

I was stunned. My heart beat fast. But suddenly I felt the Lord so near! He whispered, *Do not fear, for I am with you.* I was filled with heavenly joy. I ran into an empty room and worshiped the Lord with my face to the ground. I thanked Him for the privilege of suffering for Him.

There was a new law in Romania, though, that anyone caught without a student or working card would be arrested and put in labor camp.

"I need to find a job," I said to my father.

The city of Iaşi was full of tourist attractions and many old churches, monasteries, and museums. There was a tourist office on Piaţa Unirii, in the center of the city. They had placed an advertisement in the newspaper saying that they needed guides who could speak English.

I eagerly applied for the job. The office was a welcoming place, with clean carpets and flowers on the table.

"Could you give me a job?" I asked the elegant blond lady at the desk. "I speak English quite well."

She took my name and went away to check it on a list in the office at the back.

"We're sorry," she said when she returned. "We do not hire believers."

Not far away from the center, up a hilly street, on Gheorghe Asache, was the Institute of Medicine and Pharmacy. My sister, Aurora, was a student there. It was a huge building next to the largest children's hospital in Moldavia. They were advertising the need for specialized translators. Quickly I enrolled for the translator's examination. After studying a thick book of medical terms for a week or so, I obtained my diploma with honors. I liked the idea of working as a translator there and I was full of hope.

But soon I was to be disappointed again.

"The Securitate informed us that you have been translating in secret meetings for foreign missionaries. We cannot hire you."

I needed a working card. The police had already stopped me and asked me for it twice. I was in danger of being sent to a labor camp.

I tried several other places, but the response was always the same.

There was a sister in Iaşi called Maria Lazăr. She had a deep prayer life and could encourage many. I went to see her.

"I have been praying for you, Genovieva," she said as I entered her apartment. "The Lord told me in a dream that He would give you a job next Sunday."

I left her place wondering how I could receive a job on a Sunday. On that day I would not be traveling from business to business seeking work—I would be sitting on a bench in the church.

"We need a caretaker," Pastor Radu announced at the end of the service. "Sister Ana resigned, as she finds it too much work. As you know, there is a lot of dust and mud to clean, and we can't pay very much either. Is there anyone who wants to take the job?"

There was silence in the church. My heart started to beat fast. *Didn't you ask Me to use you?* I heard the Lord say. *Why not start here?*

I looked around. No one had volunteered. I raised my hand.

"I will."

That day I received the keys to the church, the gate, and the woodshed. I was provided with a dustpan, a broom, and cloths with which to wash the floor and windows. The thought of being all by myself with the Lord in His house filled me with joy.

I didn't know that I would spend seven years of my life there, or that I would write songs for children and start a children's choir, which was destined to become famous and have an impact on the whole country.

Chapter Two

My Family

My homeland of Romania, a country in Eastern Europe, has high mountains and plains with wheat fields. You can often see shepherds playing the flute as they watch over their sheep. In the villages, people paint their houses blue, green, mauve, or pink. Some even have flowers painted on them. People walk the muddy roads or go by horse-drawn caravans.

The towns and cities have universities and schools, with theaters and museums. There are broad sidewalks shaded by trees. The busy streets bustle with cars, trams, and buses.

In the spring, rows of lime trees spread a perfume of lemon and honey. In the summer, gardens have roses full of fragrance; out of their velvety petals, women make rose confiture, a fancy jam served to guests on little plates with a glass of cold water.

You might think that everybody is happy in such a country, but it is not so. The communists tried to make Romania an atheistic country—a land with no church, no God, and no Bible.

That made the Romanian people very sad!

I grew up in the city of Iași, in a small house with a garden and fruit trees. Our family had five children at home: Dionisie, Aurora, me, Constantin, and Teodor. Dionisie was the oldest. He had brown eyes and brown hair like mine. Aurora had auburn hair and freckles, with green eyes. Constantin was skinny and fair. Teodor had blue eyes and light brown hair. We were all different, but got on well together, especially at playing games.

One warm spring day, my mother was cooking outside, at her brick stove in the shade of a walnut tree. She was a small, stocky woman who constantly kept busy, cleaning, sewing, washing, and cooking.

"I will butcher two chickens and I'll make a delicious borscht especially for Sunday," she said. Her dark eyes gave each of us a look that promised we would be expected to help prepare the meal. Sure enough, after she smoothed her apron over her dress and tightened her scarf over her long, black braid, her next words were, "I will need your help, children."

Soon we all gathered around her and helped pull off the feathers and wash the meat. Aurora peeled the potatoes. Mother cut the carrots and the onions very fine. I picked fragrant herbs from our garden—green parsley, dill, and sage—and brought them to my mother. Dionisie gathered wood for the fire. Soon the soup was boiling in the large cooking pot. Mother loved that pot, even though it didn't have a lid.

My mother knew how to make the borscht just right, seasoned with lemon juice and herbs. Soon it was ready and our mouths were watering.

"Look what I found," Dionisie announced. "A bottle of perfume." He was eleven, and he was curious about everything. Especially things he shouldn't be playing with.

"Let me take a look," I asked.

"Let me smell it!" Aurora pleaded.

"Me too, me too!" Constantin and Teodor screamed.

"I will open it and let each one smell it," Dionisie said, jumping up and down as all the children's hands grabbed at the bottle. "But I want it back."

Splash! The open bottle of perfume landed in the cooking pot. We children froze, watching in horror as the perfume spilled from the bottle and mixed in with the soup.

Mother tasted the soup. "You spoiled my borscht," she scolded. "Now I have to throw it away."

She gave Dionisie a good spanking.

Father had just come in from work. "Don't throw it away," he said. "I will eat it. Everything tastes good when you are hungry. If only I had this soup when I was in hiding from the Nazis...."

For a whole week, my father ate perfumed borscht. He never said a word about it to Dionisie.

My father seemed to be a big man, though he was not tall. But there was something big about the way he wore his wide trousers suspended by braces, and something brave about his nearly bald head. Maybe this was because he had lost most of his curly brown hair while sick and starving, in hiding from the Nazis. His eyes were brown and lively, and his nose large and pointed. To me, he was big in every way that was important.

My father was a Jew who believed that Jesus was the Messiah. Though he was forced to live in great poverty because of his faith, he was always joyful. He treated his enemies with respect and humor and prayed for them.

Every morning my mother gave him two baked potatoes to take to work for lunch. The rich communist ladies in his office loved him. They would sometimes secretly replace his lunch with their expensive meat sandwiches.

"Police!" my father would shout, while the ladies roared with laughter. "Police! They stole my potatoes!"

My father used to play the violin, mandolin, and other instruments. For several years, he had been the assistant conductor of the Philharmonic Orchestra in Iaşi. My mother said she fell in love with him when she heard him play the harp. He tried to get each one of us to play at least one musical instrument. I learned to play the mandolin well.

Once he came home with an old famous Steiner violin he had found in a secondhand shop. He tried it and it sounded beautiful, but my mother scolded him.

"You spent my grocery money! Now, I will not have enough for food."

She went on at him for a few minutes, at which he would bite his lips and say to himself with a smile, "Don't answer back, Nicolae. Shut up!"

While she was still flustered, he sat down on the bed and we heard a loud *crack*. He had sat down on the violin. Then my mother started to laugh and so did the rest of us. He repaired it, but it never sounded the same.

Our house was often watched by the secret police. They would have loved to catch my parents holding a prayer meeting. Then they could have fined them or put them in prison.

One rainy, chilly evening, about nine o'clock, my mother had just come in from shutting the hens in the henhouse.

"Culiţă," she said. "There is a raincoat on one of our vines. I wonder if the wind might have brought it, or…what?"

"A raincoat?" my father asked. "Let's have a look.… I could do with one."

He went out in the back of the garden and we all followed him.

"There," he said. But as he got hold of it, a man jumped up from underneath it and ran away. My father ran after him and we all followed him.

"Stop! I am going to shoot you! Bang! Bang!" my father shouted jokingly, while pursuing him.

The secret policeman jumped over the fence. We jumped over too, shouting, "Stop! I am going to shoot you! Bang! Bang!"

The agent disappeared into the night and we turned back. My father found one of his shoes in the fence. He wrapped it with the raincoat in a newspaper and took the parcel the next morning to the secret police station.

"I surprised a thief last night in my back yard. It should be easy for you to identify him from these," he told the officer on duty.

"Leave them here, Mr. Sfatcu!" he said, embarrassed.

After that my father was careful what he said in the house. He shared sensitive things only as he walked with us in the street or in the park.

In the evenings at home, we often played as an orchestra, and my mother hummed along. We also prayed together, and my father read to us from the Bible. To worship the Lord was risky, but that was the secret of our strength as a family.

Chapter Three

The Candy Cone

on't forget the flowers," my mother shouted after me as I ran out of the house on my first day of school.

With my schoolbag on my back, I went into the front garden and picked red roses and white and yellow chrysanthemums. I made a lovely bouquet, which I was supposed to give to my teacher, Comrade Cireş.

Here I was, getting ready to start school on September 15, 1958. I was seven and a half years old, small and dark with long brown hair, braided in two tails. I wore my school uniform, a blue pinafore dress with a white apron, and I had a yellow number 803 attached to my sleeve. I couldn't enter the school without this number, and I was supposed to wear it wherever I went.

The school was a brick building with communist flags in the front and a big slogan that read: *Trăiască Partidul Comunist Român!* which meant "Long live the Romanian Communist Party!" This was General School Number 23, Târguşorul Copou. I joined the hundreds of children in the playground.

Soon the bell rang and all the children were led to their classrooms. I entered a classroom with wooden floors and three rows of benches, ready to accommodate the thirty-nine children.

"What is your name?" the teacher asked me as he took my flowers. He was big and tall, with small dark eyes and a pink round face.

"Sfatcu Genovieva," I replied.

"I will take you to your seat," he said and led me straight to the far left corner in the back of the classroom. "This is Rudi Popolov, your bench-mate. You will sit here with your hands to the back, except for when you read or write. You are not allowed to speak with each other."

I never said a word to Rudi, that Jewish boy. Neither did he ever speak to me. There were empty benches around us, to keep us isolated from the rest of the class. Why? Because we came from families who worshiped the God of Israel and honored His Word. Children from Christian families all over the country were treated the same way.

For the next four years, hardly anybody spoke to me or played with me.

In the next months, I learned to read and write very well. My note-books were put in the school exhibition as an example of beautiful hand-writing. However, instead of putting my name under them, the teachers put the name of Patraşcu Octavian, a child from a communist family. When I saw that, I was very upset. My father comforted me, "When you grow up, whose writing will be beautiful? Yours! Nobody will be able to take your handwriting from you."

I was a good student, but that didn't make any difference to Comrade Cireş. He was a communist and hated Jews and Christians. During the breaks, while the children were outside playing, several times he came to me and beat me with his fists, pulling my hair and my ears in his fury, without telling me why.

Once, Comrade Cireş came to me at the back of the classroom.

"Stand up and put out your right hand," he ordered. Then he hit my palm with a long wooden ruler, again and again. I cried but nobody came to my rescue. He did the same to Rudi.

"The left palm now," he shouted. I handed my other palm to be beaten. My hands became so swollen that I could hardly write.

After one of these beatings, my father turned up unexpectedly at school and saw my red swollen hands. His eyes clashed for a long time with Comrade Cireş' eyes.

On the way home, holding me tenderly by the hand, my father said, "This man killed many Jews in Hitler's time. And he was never punished."

"I don't like him," I said.

"I know. But Jesus told us to love our enemies and pray for them. And don't forget, Jesus will reward you one day for this, because He said, 'Blessed are those who are persecuted....'"

He kissed my hands many times, and he was so kind to me that soon I forgot all my troubles—at least till the next day.

And so I endured my first year of school.

When I was in the second grade, we had student teachers: two girls and a young man. They sat at the back of our class for the whole term. They took pity on me, seeing how isolated and punished I was. At the end of term, they secretly brought a bag of candies to school. During the break, they approached me at the back of the classroom where I was sitting with my hands to my back. They each bent over me and gave me a hug. Then they put a large brown shiny paper cone full of candies next to my schoolbag under the bench. I thought nobody saw them.

"Hide it," they said. "It is for you."

I felt my face blush with excitement, and I beamed at them. I smelled the milk candies and couldn't wait to taste one.

When the bell rang, I put my schoolbag on my back and went out as fast as I could, holding the candy cone tight under my right arm. I was out of the gate, passing the school grounds, and I hurried my steps. When I thought I was safe, I held my cone of candies in front of me so I could decide which one to eat first. But then I heard steps behind me and voices shouting, "Stop! Sfatcu, stop! Stop, stinking Jew!"

It was Lucius Dumitrescu and Raul Vulcănescu, the sons of high communist officials. They caught me by my back and fought for the candies.

"No!" I screamed, holding the cone with all my strength. They twisted my arm and the cone fell to the ground, candies rolling everywhere. They quickly gathered up the candies, put them back in the cone, and ran back to school, where they handed the cone to Comrade Cireş. With a smile of satisfaction on his face and his arms folded, he had watched from the schoolyard as his orders were carried out.

I cried all the way home. When I arrived, my mother was making pancakes and my brothers and sister were playing in the garden. My father told me, "'In all things God works for the good of those who love him' (Romans 8:28). One day, you will see, God will bring a blessing out of this sad story."

But all I could think of was that my candy cone had been taken from me by force. What blessing could result from that?

Chapter Four

The Christmas Guest

Whose turn is it to come with me to church?" my father asked us five children one day.

"Mine," I said and quickly put on my long brown velvet dress, which I had earned by babysitting for Zuzu, the child of a rich communist family. I slipped into my rubber boots and put on my winter coat with a hood, which my mother had made.

In Romania if you worshiped God, you were poor and in danger. If you worshiped the president, all was well with you.

Children like me had school every day, even on Sundays. I had to be at the Pioneers' House, a place where young communists got together, from nine until twelve. In that way, pupils were hindered from going to church. We were taught that God did not exist and we were forced to sing glory to the Communist Party, and to worship the president of Romania. But my father tried hard to keep the five of us in touch with the church. He would take us, one by one, to all sorts of meetings occurring during the week, or on Sunday evenings, while my mother took care of the housekeeping.

On that December evening in 1960, it was snowing in Iaşi. It felt good to be inside the church on Strada Sărărie, where a warm fire burned in the stove. It was the Monday night prayer meeting. I was nine years old at the time, and I understood more and more about the persecution of Christians in our country. Our rights were being taken away one after another. Even the giving of gifts was controlled by the secret police.

The church was fairly empty, as many were at work that evening. Some thirty brothers sat on the benches on the left-hand side, and about the same number of sisters sat on the right. The fresh scent of fir wafted from the Christmas tree in the front right corner. It was decorated with silver balls and candies wrapped in red and yellow foil. Nuts and apples hung from its branches. My father played the pump organ just in front of the tree, and brother Florea led the service from behind a small table in front of the pulpit. He was a middle-aged man dressed in an elegant suit and tie, with wavy brown hair. My father had told me that there were some in the church who were informers for the secret police. I sometimes wondered who they were.

While we were singing "Silent Night," the door opened and in came an old woman dressed in black with a shawl and a large scarf around her head. She was all covered in snow. As she took a seat next to me, I noticed that her old cotton shoes were wet through. She was trembling with cold, and looked tired as she took off her patched coat and scarf to let them dry near the stove.

"It's sister Dorina, from Bârlad," someone whispered, recognizing her. "She suffered much for her faith."

First, a passage of Scripture was read and then it was the prayer time. Then all the brothers and sisters prayed in succession, one after another. After the offering was taken, sister Dorina stood up. As she started to speak everyone stared at her.

"Greetings in the name of the Lord Jesus! I am just passing through the area. I am in great need of one hundred *lei* for my train ticket home. Please help me if you can."

There was silence in the church.

After a while Florea announced, "Excuse me, it is against the law to give gifts without authorization. We could be arrested for it."

I remembered how my father had taught us always to give to the poor.

"If a beggar knocks at your door asking for bread," he said, "and you have only one slice, give him half of it. And if someone asks you for money and you have ten pennies, give him five. Then the Lord will bless you!"

"And what if you don't have any money?" I had asked him.

"Then you can give a kind word, a smile, or a hug. Love always has something to give."

Sister Dorina sat down, her eyes closed. She was praying silently.

"She belongs to an illegal church," Florea's wife commented. She was sitting at the back, dressed in a fur coat. "If we help someone who is in trouble with the authorities, we ourselves will get into trouble. They can take our jobs, fine us, and even close the church."

"I put all I had in the offering," a man said from the left-hand side. "I'm sorry I can't help her."

"Why can't we do what we want with our offerings?" said a sister in a low voice.

Other muffled voices could be heard from the congregation.

Hearing all this, sister Dorina said, "I'm sorry. I didn't mean to trouble you. I will walk home."

"We can't let her walk," my father spoke up. "It's sixty miles to Bârlad. Let's take a second offering and see what we can come up with."

My father had been so persecuted for his faith that his salary was just a fraction of what others received. I knew he had hardly anything, and most of the others didn't have that amount of money either.

"We can't take a second offering," Florea intervened. "All offerings have to be approved by the union in Bucharest. Anyway, love offerings for guests like her are illegal."

At this sister Dorina stood up again and put on her coat and scarf. "It's all right, I will walk," she said.

She bent down to tie the laces of her worn-out shoes.

I looked at my father. His chin was trembling, and he had tears in his eyes. I started to cry too. By this time the church was singing the closing song.

She will go out in the snow and walk miles and miles through the fields and forests, I thought. *The wind will blow in her face and she will get weaker and weaker and freeze to death.*

"You are dismissed," I heard Florea say after the closing prayer.

Everything seemed lost.

I watched Florea as he put the counted offering in an envelope, which he then put in his case. I suddenly knew what I had to do. I went straight up to him, took hold of his sleeve, and started to cry aloud, "Please, help her! She is so poor!"

"Go to your place, Genovieva, that's not nice."

"Please," I said crying even louder and tightening my hold on his sleeve with both hands.

"Leave me alone, little girl," he said, trying to shake me off.

By now everyone watched as they put on their coats at the back of the church. Sister Dorina was among them. Florea was getting embarrassed.

"Please, help her!" I kept on crying, keeping hold of his sleeve.

He pinched my left cheek as hard as he could to make me let go of his sleeve, but I didn't. Suddenly he changed his mind. He took a hundred *lei* out of the offering envelope and walked over to sister Dorina and gave it to her. Then he and his wife hurried out of the church.

Soon everyone had left except my father and sister Dorina. While my father locked the door and the gate, sister Dorina gave me a hug.

"Thank you, little girl. God bless you! May you become a missionary when you grow up," she said. Then she went to the railway station to catch her train.

My father and I were both happy as we walked home through the snow. It was cold, but I didn't feel it, because joy warmed up my whole being. I was glad that a small girl like me could make a difference in another person's life. Was that the blessing my father had told me about when the boys stole my candies? I was thankful we weren't caught…this time.

Chapter Five

Miriam, the Orphan Girl

The years passed and I grew up and finished high school. From there I went to the Alexandru Ioan Cuza University in Iaşi to study English.

Over the years my family home remained open to any Christian believer who was in trouble. Anyone who was in need received encouragement, a bed for the night, or a plate of food.

When I gave my life to the Lord, He filled my heart with joy, courage, and love. I wanted to tell all those around me about His salvation so that they might become happy too. I witnessed about Jesus to anyone I met. I also witnessed about the Savior in hospitals and on buses and trains. One day a friend told me, "There is a girl in my village living in a hut all by herself. She is an orphan and very sick. Could you come and tell her about Jesus?"

"I will try," I said. "Doesn't the Bible say that pure religion is to take care of orphans?"

One evening that summer I took a bus and went to Vânători, a village five miles north of Iaşi. Teodor, my brother, came along. When we arrived there, we entered the one-room hut. The small window was shaded by a fir tree. There was a low three-legged table with two stools in the small room, and a stove with old ashes in a corner. There, on a narrow bed, lay Miriam.

"I brought you some flowers," I said, giving her a hug. Then I took a seat next to her.

Miriam nodded. "Thank you." She had a white face, brown eyes, and short brown hair.

"Here are some apples," said Teodor.

"Your friend Eugenia told me about you," I said. "I am so glad she did."

"She is so kind to me. She brings me soup every day and bread and water. I wish someone would change my bandage," said Miriam, sitting up in her bed. "My arm hurts me very badly."

"I will do that for you," I said, taking courage. I washed her arm and changed her bandage.

"How long have you lived in this hut?" Teodor asked.

"Since the spring, when they discharged me from the orphanage in Sculeni. They didn't have room for me there. This hut once belonged to my grandmother. The doctor said I had terminal cancer. So they brought me here to die."

"Don't you have any family?" I asked, heartbroken.

"No, nobody ever came to see me. All my life I was in that children's home, on the Soviet border, a few miles from here."

"Did anybody ever tell you about Jesus?" I asked her.

"Yes, a monk by the name of Gherasim. He was a kind man. He was the only one who told us about the Savior."

"I know him," I said.

"There was a wire fence all around the orphanage," Miriam continued. "Nobody was allowed to come near to see us. Police guarded the place. Brother Gherasim used to hide in the forest across the street. When the police went away for a break, he came to the fence. We rushed to the fence and stretched out our hands to receive candies from him. Then he told us about God. I wonder where he is now."

I knew where Gherasim was, but I didn't want to upset the girl. One day he had been caught telling orphans about Jesus. As a punishment he was put in prison. He came out after six months and was now living in hiding in the mountains.

"Brother Gherasim told us about a place called Paradise," said Miriam. "A wonderful place prepared for all children, including orphans. I wish so much to go there! I am in great pain. At night I hear the dogs barking and owls hooting. Then I am so afraid that something evil will come and take me away."

"Don't be afraid," I said, holding her hand. "If you give your heart to Jesus, He promises to be with you every moment. He will never leave you alone. Would you like to pray and confess Him as your personal Savior?"

"Yes, I would."

"Then repeat after me: Lord Jesus Christ, I believe You died for me."

"Lord Jesus Christ, I believe You died for me."

"Your blood was shed for me, for the forgiveness of my sins."

"Your blood was shed for me, for the forgiveness of my sins."

"Please make me Your child and take me to Paradise."

"Please make me Your child and take me to Paradise."

Then Miriam lay down on her pillow and fell asleep. Her eyes were half-open toward the ceiling. She was taking short, deep breaths.

"Is she dying?" I asked Teodor, and couldn't help crying.

"Her pulse is very slow," he said, holding her hand.

Ox-drawn carts passed slowly on the road. The evening was falling, and I lit the gas lamp on the wall. An owl was hooting in the fir tree, which, they say, bodes death.

There was silence in the hut and the smell of burning kerosene. I was silently praying for Miriam.

Suddenly she woke up and opened her eyes. She sat up in bed smiling.

"I saw two angels," she said. "They had wings, bright clothes, and shining faces. They smiled at me. One of them said, 'Miriam, don't be afraid. Soon we will take you to a beautiful garden, and there you will take care of flowers. Many friends are waiting for you there. You will be so happy!' Then they disappeared. I have so much joy and I'm not afraid anymore!"

It was late when we left Miriam, and no buses were running. We had to walk five miles back home. But I was so happy that it did not matter.

I went to see Miriam again. Shortly afterward, she died and went to that beautiful garden, prepared by God for orphans, where children are happy forever.

I knew that there were many orphans in Romania, and how much I desired to help them!

Chapter Six

A Price to Pay

The University of Iași was housed in an enormous stone building with elegant sculptures and statues and a large flight of steps in front. It was located in the most beautiful district of the city, the wooded hill of Copou. There was fierce competition to get in, and I was proud to be one of its thousands of students. Then, one autumn morning I was called to the office.

"Miss Genovieva Sfatcu!" announced the secretary, "you are expelled from this university, and you are not allowed to enter any other institute of higher education in the country. It is because of your Christian activities."

I was stunned. My heart beat fast. But suddenly I felt the Lord so near! He whispered, *Do not fear, for I am with you.* I was filled with heavenly joy. I ran into an empty room and worshiped the Lord with my face to the ground. I thanked Him for the privilege of suffering for Him.

There was a new law in Romania, though, that anyone caught without a working card in the street would be arrested and put in labor camp on charges of parasitism.

I applied for jobs as an English-speaking guide at the tourist office and as a translator at the Institute of Medicine and Pharmacy, but my applications were rejected.

"I need to find a job," I said to my father.

"Let's go to the chemical factory," he suggested. "The director there is an old friend of mine."

From our small house on Strada Coşbuc to the bus station in the center was a walk of about three miles. People were used to walking a lot, carrying books or groceries in their bags. The sidewalks were wide, lined with roses and shaded by lime trees. I loved my father and was so happy to have this time with him. I took his arm and we walked to the center, where we were going to catch a bus to the other end of the city.

"Never complain to anyone about what has happened," he said as we walked. "Also, love your enemies. Don't forget that, Genovieva."

How good it was that he gave me this advice! I was going to need it, as I would have many enemies.

"We are being followed," my father whispered suddenly, squeezing my hand.

I turned around discreetly and caught a glimpse of the man.

We got on the bus and so did he. The bus traveled by the Palace of Culture, along the Bahlui River, and past hundreds of apartment blocks.

Soon we were out of town and got off. The chemical factory was full of smoke. I didn't like the smell, the gray walls, and the abandoned area around it. But that was not important. All I wanted was a job and the security of having a working card. When my father and the director of the factory met, they hugged each other many times, smiling and joking. I could see that the director liked my father, and I hoped that he would help me. I filled out the application form.

But soon the same man came back to us without a smile.

"They say your daughter tried to help a Christian in prison, or something like that. She is blacklisted. I cannot hire her."

There was a botanical garden five minutes' walk up the street from my house, and I decided I would apply for a job there. It was a beautiful place with many walnut trees and weeping willows. There were also exotic plants in greenhouses and all sorts of flowers and bushes outside. They needed manual workers, and I would have loved to be one of them.

I knocked at the door of the director's office.

"Come in."

I entered an expensive room with a Persian carpet on the floor. The director, a middle-aged man in an elegant suit, was a professor of horticulture at the Institute up the road.

"Can you give me a job?" I asked.

He looked at me. "Well…it is true that we badly need manual workers. Would you be ready to dig holes for flowers and trees?"

"Yes, anything."

"Fill out this form. I will hire you," he said.

In three days I was back in his office to start my new job. The same well-dressed man received me in the same office.

"I was informed that you make converts to Jesus Christ in villages and hospitals. I would not be allowed to hire you even if I wanted to. But I would gladly give you some money if you could teach me English."

"Thank you very much, but I need a working card. The police have already stopped me and asked me for it twice. I am in danger of being sent to a labor camp."

I tried several other places, but the response was always the same.

There was a sister in Iaşi called Maria Lazăr, who was a secret Christian. She had a deep prayer life and could encourage many. I went to see her.

"I have been praying for you," she said as I entered her apartment. "The Lord told me in a dream that He would give you a job next Sunday."

I left her place, wondering how I could receive a job on a Sunday. On that day I would be sitting on a bench, worshiping God in the church.

"We need a caretaker," Pastor Radu announced at the end of the service. "Sister Ana resigned, as she finds it too much work. As you know, there is a lot of dust and mud to clean, and we can't pay very much either. Is there anyone who wants to take the job?"

There was silence in the church. My heart started to beat fast. *Didn't you ask Me to use you?* I heard the Lord say. *Why not start here?*

I looked around. No one had volunteered. I raised my hand.

"I will."

That day I received the keys to the church, the gate, and the woodshed. I was provided with a dustpan, a broom, and cloths with which to wash the floor and windows. When I realized I would be all by myself with the Lord in His house, I was filled with joy!

But I didn't imagine that the secret police were going to try to hinder me even in this.

An application was made by the elders of the church to the Baptist Union in Bucharest. The union president sent back the following reply signed by him: "We do not believe that a girl like Genovieva with scholastic education should stoop to the level of a caretaker. We advise her to seek a more suitable job."

"He didn't understand," I said to the pastor. "A girl like me with scholastic education will soon end up in labor camp! I'm sure that if we send the application back with a letter explaining the situation, he will help me."

The new application was sent back to Bucharest. But exactly the same answer came back.

Maybe the new president will be more courageous, I said to myself when the president of the Baptist Union changed later on. A third application was mailed. But the same answer came back, signed by the new president. What was I going to do now?

One day as I was walking through the center of town, someone stopped me in the street. I recognized him immediately. He was the man who had followed my father and me to the chemical factory. He lived down the road from us and worked for the secret police. I often saw him coming home with bags full of foods available only in the Communist Party shops: oranges, Greek olives, Swiss cheese, Italian salami. All we could get were stale bread and spoiled potatoes.

"Miss Genovieva," he said, taking my hand and kissing it, "don't try in vain. Absolutely no one will give you a job. Don't you understand it is *us* behind it?"

I looked at him. He was a young man with fair hair, red cheeks, and cold blue eyes.

"The Lord will help me," I said.

"Listen!" he answered. "I was in the meeting when things were decided. But there is one job you *can* have, even tomorrow, if you cooperate. It is very well paid and no one will bother you anymore. Because you speak English so well, we could employ you in the censorship office of the secret police."

I looked him in the eye and said, "I would rather starve than work for you, Mr. Bâcu."

"You will be sorry," he mumbled and quickly turned away.

"Lord," I prayed, "I am in great trouble. Please, help me!"

Soon the elders of the church—my father among them—made a courageous decision. They typed out a paper that said, "We, the elders of the Baptist Church, hire Genovieva as a daily caretaker. She will be here four hours a day to clean and to open and close the doors. This paper is signed by us, the elders, and stamped with the church stamp."

How happy I was when I held in my hands this work contract! As long as I was in the church, this paper protected me from being taken to labor camp. But was it going to cover me in the streets as well? Soon I was going to find out.

Chapter Seven

In the House of the Lord

A re you all right, Genovieva?" my father asked me as we met at the church door. At almost sixty, he was bald and broad-shouldered. His faith was like a rock and we were very fond of each other. "We expected you home last night."

"I slept here at the church," I replied. "I would like to stay here from now on, if that's OK with the elders. With policemen hiding behind every tree, it's too dangerous for me to walk three miles back and forth every day."

My father held my hand. "What happened?"

"On Monday, after I had cleaned the church, I went out. A policeman was hiding behind a pillar down the street. He stopped me and asked me for my working card. I handed him the contract stamped by the church to prove I was hired as a daily cleaning lady."

"And…?"

"He looked at the paper and said, 'This is not an official working card. I suspect you are one of those vagabonds. Your place is in labor camp!'"

"Those criminals!" my father exclaimed.

"Well, the Lord delivered me out of his hands. But I will try to stay off the streets as much as possible."

"I will speak with Pastor Radu to see if you could use the little room where we keep the church archives," he suggested. My father had been one of the founders of the Baptist Church in our city and was still one of its elders. "When you go out, try to be with at least one other person. They don't like to make public arrests, you know."

The city of Iași spread its streets over seven hills. Some hills were covered with trees, and others had parks like the Copou Hill, where my family home was situated. Sărărie Hill was more densely populated than Copou Hill, two miles away. There were houses with gardens on both sides of Strada Sărărie, which went up the hill for over three miles. The church was on the right-hand side as you walked up from Golia Tower.

I began living at the church in February, 1973. As long as I was there I felt safe. The secret police were not usually allowed to disturb a place of worship. But the building was not fit to be lived in. The church, which accommodated over three hundred people on Sundays, was badly in need of repair. However, no repairs were allowed without authorization. The poor elders would wait for years for a permit that would never come.

I thought I would be there for a few months, until the Lord opened some other door for me. Little did I know that I would spend seven years of my life there.

"As far as I am concerned, you can live in the little office," Pastor Radu said as we talked in the yard one morning. "Here is the key."

He had become pastor after the previous one was deported to Maramureş. Pastor Radu was in his mid-forties, short and stocky, with blue eyes that sparkled when he laughed. He had three small children whom I grew to know and love during the time I lived at the church.

"There is a woolen quilt and some pillows," he continued. "Sister Lazăr gave them to me when her mother died. Feel free to use them."

"Thank you," I said as he left.

I locked the gate and remained all by myself at the church. The fence was tall enough to give me a sense of privacy and protection.

I went down the side of the church to the archive room and I opened the door. It was a small dark room with cobwebs on the walls and a musty smell. There was a barred window on the right and a heavy iron cupboard on the left, in which the archives were kept locked. There was a bed opposite the door and a table with an old typewriter and a telephone. Under the table I found some dry bread and some grape juice left over from the communion. That was to be my first meal there.

It was a cold winter day and it started to snow. Little snowflakes got in through the door and window, which didn't shut properly. Icy air came in through the long cracks in the wall.

If I want to get any sleep tonight I'll have to do something about this place, I thought.

I started to clean the little office. Under the old, damp carpet, I found layers of newspaper eaten by mice. I carried them out and swept the cement floor clean. I took the carpet out, shook it, and put it back. Soon all the cobwebs were gone. I filled the cracks with newspaper. Then I brought in some fir branches from the garden and hung them on the walls. I found an old electric heater without a plug. My brother, Costică, had shown me how to plug wires directly into a socket. I tried, taking much care not to touch the metal wires, and the heater worked. Soon my little room was warm and smelled of fir.

I knelt and thanked the Lord for my new home. Suddenly the Lord filled my heart with indescribable joy. I read the Bible and prayed for hours. The Lord was there with me, I had no doubt about it.

One day a friend came to see me.

"How nice you've made this little room!" Rebeca said. She was a student in Iaşi, at the Institute of Chemistry. "Can we use it for prayer meetings on Sunday mornings?"

"Of course," I said.

"We will call it the 'Golden Room,'" said Slavka, another girl from the church.

And it remained the "Golden Room" for the years to come.

My new job kept me busy. I had to cut wood in the orchard behind the church and carry it in. Then I had to make the fire and keep it burning on the days when there were services. That included Sundays all day, and Monday, Wednesday, Friday, and Saturday evenings. Every week several hundred people came, and when it was wet, they brought in mud. After every meeting I had to sweep and carry out the mud. Then I had to bring water from the back of the church and wash the floor with cold water and soda. My hands swelled and reddened. I also had to take the aisle carpet out every week, and the one from under the pulpit. I would put them on a line and beat them with a carpet beater. There was a lot of dusting to do all the time. I also had to prepare the communion and wash the little glasses afterward. There were flower vases to change and the yard to keep in order.

The telephone was a great comfort. Not many Christians had a phone. *If I need help, I can quickly call the pastor or the Stan family*, I thought. *I know they would come to my rescue at any time.*

But this comfort would soon be taken away.

One day in March, two secret policemen came to the church and confronted me.

"We have orders to cut the telephone wires," Lieutenant Negru said. He was a tall man, with blond hair and dark glasses. "You cannot be trusted with such a thing. You are an enemy of the country." The other man didn't speak, but took away the phone and cut the wire outside with a pair of pliers.

After they left, I knelt down and consecrated my life to the Lord anew. I prayed, "Lord, when I am in trouble, I will call upon You. I'm so glad nobody can cut my line to You."

At the church I had four neighbors. The old couple living opposite the church was kind, but reserved. Next to them, down the street, a woman spied on me all the time from behind her curtain. Only at night did she stop. Up the street from the church, on my side, behind a high wooden fence, lived a rich family. They were all members of the Communist Party and were notorious secret police informers. They kept large dogs that barked at any noise. Next to the church down the street lived Mr. Balif, an old man from the former royal family. He lived with his sister in an old house. He was not a Christian, but he hated the communists with all his heart. One day he called me to the fence to talk, looking up and down all the time to make sure nobody overheard our conversation.

"Listen, Miss Genovieva," he said. "The secret police asked me to spy on you. I can see your life is in danger. I would like to help you. I am going to make some hidden steps for you in the fence, and I will hang a rope from the tree to help you over if you ever need to run."

Oh, how useful those steps and that rope were going to be!

I was happy living in the little room, but soon this happiness was to be taken from me.

One day the Inspector of Cults, Inspector Andronic, came to the church. He brought the pastor with him.

"Genovieva," said Inspector Andronic. "I came to tell you that you are not allowed to live in this office. Get all your things out and give the bedding back to the pastor. If we ever catch you sleeping there again, the church will be in big trouble!"

Pastor Radu was very sad as he took his comforter and pillows, which I would never see again. After they left I knelt for a long time. I needed to be reassured of the Lord's protection and love in that place. Now it was the beginning of April, and it was starting to warm up.

Where should I sleep tonight? I wondered.

Suddenly I knew. There was a woodshed attached to the back of the church. It was built on logs, two feet above the ground. I climbed the four stairs and opened the padlock on the tall, flimsy door. Inside was the church baptistery. The long, narrow room was dark, the only light coming from the window in the top of the door. There were only a thick velvet curtain and a board separating the church from the woodshed.

I looked at the ugly place and shivered. *How am I ever going to sleep here with all these bugs and who knows what else?*

Suddenly I heard a noise and I dashed out in fear. *Pock! Pock!* I listened, praying for protection. Then I heard it again: *Pock! Pock!* I listened. It was coming from rats. They were crawling from underneath, climbing up to the ceiling, and jumping on the floor.

"Get out of here!" I shouted, chasing them with my broom. "From now on this is my place." But they didn't listen, and even worse, they were not afraid of me.

That afternoon a friend came to see me.

"Maria," I told her, "please bring me some rat poison." She was from an underground church and she knew the Lord well.

"Let's pray first," she advised me. "The Lord can command any creature to come or to go. We will see if we need the poison or not."

We prayed and after two or three days all the rats left. They never returned. I was so happy that God had answered our prayer. I felt the Lord so close!

I worked hard to wash the walls and the floor with a brush. Soon it started to rain and I could see that it would be hard to stop it from coming in. Out of tree stumps and planks I made a rough bed. For a covering, I could use some old, thin curtains.

One day a friend brought me some dry beans. I found a pot and made a fire outside to try to cook them. It was hard to cook, so I preferred to eat bread, fruit, and vegetables. My food was going to be simple.

I learned to wash my hair with cold water or sometimes water heated by the sun. I washed my skirt with a hose and let it dry on me.

One day a team from abroad brought me an important proposal: "Would you be willing to receive Bibles and distribute them?"

"Yes," I answered without hesitation.

It was dangerous work, but I had no doubt I was ready to risk my life to distribute the Word of God.

About every three weeks after that, I received loads of Bibles by night at the church. It was pitch dark, and there were many hiding places. Now I knew why the Lord had brought me to live at the church.

The joy of the Lord filled my being, and I told Him that I wanted to serve Him all my life. I felt His presence in the woodshed and was so happy! The words of Jesus from John 14:23 were so real to me: "If anyone loves me.… My Father will love him, and we will come to him and make our home with him."

I started a Sunday school in that woodshed for the children. I taught them Bible stories and how to pray. Many gave their lives to the Lord. The woodshed was full of children every Sunday. It remained their meeting place for many years to come.

I wrote songs and started a children's choir, never suspecting that later on they would have an impact on the whole country.

Soon my joy was threatened again. The police came to the woodshed, accompanied by witnesses. Pastor Radu was called as well.

"Get all your things out," the policeman shouted. "You are not allowed to live here. If we catch you sleeping here again, we will close the church."

I gathered all my things and put them in a plastic bag.

"My job is threatened because of you," Pastor Radu told me after the police had left. "They are angry with you for starting the work with the children. They asked me to disband it. But I can't do that," he said with a gentle smile.

I continued to see my family two or three times a week, when they came to church. They were happy to see me alive and free. The secret police threatened anyone who tried to receive me in his home.

One day the elders told me confidentially, "You can sleep at the church as long as we don't know anything about it. We are glad of your work with the children. But we prefer not to know where you sleep."

After that nobody ever asked me where I slept, or what I ate. But the Lord knew, and His grace was sufficient.

It was now September. I had been chased away from the little room and from the woodshed. *Where would I sleep now?* The shed in the orchard came to mind, but it was not properly enclosed. It was nice weather, so for the next few nights I slept on the roof. A big walnut tree covered me. I looked through its branches at the starry sky. I gave myself completely over to the Lord again, and He filled my heart with joy.

Oh, how much the secret police tried to separate me from the church! One day they changed their tactics and attacked my job.

Trouble came through a sister I hardly knew. She said, "I hear you didn't get your working card. The inspector told me to apply for the cleaning job. They told me if I started early enough, the Baptist Union would give me a pension when I retire."

I felt pain in my heart and I asked the Lord for wisdom.

"Why don't you try the job first, to see if you like it?" I suggested. "The sister that cleaned the church before me simply gave up because it was too hard for her. You are not that young either…"

She agreed to clean the church that week under my supervision. The Lord was with me and He sent rain all that week. The church floor got so dirty that it looked like a pigsty after every service.

"Keep your job, Genovieva," she said at the end of that week. "I don't want it."

Oh, how happy I was when she left and how many thanks I offered to the Lord!

One day my father came to me and said, "I had a dream, my dear, and I am very concerned for you. I dreamed that "brother" Mircea threw you into a deep pit, and you were crying to me for help. But I couldn't do anything and I was brokenhearted. Let's pray that whatever Satan plans through this dangerous man would come to nothing."

Next Sunday I understood the dream. There was a members' meeting after the morning service and many were present, including children. In the middle of it all, "brother" Mircea stood up and said, "I propose that the church eliminate the position of cleaning lady and the money paid to Genovieva be given to the poor. I myself volunteer to clean the church and hope others will join me."

There was perfect silence in the church. It had taken everyone by surprise and had been well planned by the secret police through this so-called brother. I went out to the woodshed as tears came uncontrollably to my eyes. The children crowded to comfort me and cried with me.

That week I spend much time in prayer, asking the Lord to save my job.

One afternoon Mircea came with his wife to clean the church. I went into the garden and waited. It took them several hours just to beat the carpets. They sneezed and coughed and got very angry. Nobody else came to help, and they soon gave up.

After that I decided that every month I would give back to the church three hundred *lei* out of my miserable salary of four hundred. I kept only one hundred *lei*, which was enough to buy bread. I made it public by writing my name and the sum on my tithe envelope. I continued doing this for the rest of my time there. The Lord blessed the bread I ate and it tasted sweet in my mouth.

When it turned cold at night, sleeping on the roof had to end. *Where shall I sleep?* I wondered. A Scripture verse came to mind: "Even the sparrow has found a home, and the swallow a nest for herself…a place near your altar" (Psalm 84:3).

Suddenly I knew. I was going to sleep in the church, in the main hall, near the altar. But it had to be secret. In the evenings after everybody went home, I drew the curtains, turned off the lights, locked the door and the gate, and walked down the street. A few yards down the street, instead of turning right, I would turn left and secretly make my way back to the church across my kind neighbor's garden. Under the cover of darkness I would head straight for the oak tree covered in ivy, take hold of the rope, and using the hidden steps, climb over the fence. From there I would enter the church through a back door I had left open.

I slept in the main hall of the church behind the pulpit or on a bench. Many times I covered myself with the velvet cloth from the communion table. I had to make myself very small for the cloth to cover my body. Other times I used a window curtain. But I made sure that if the police came at any time there was no trace of a bed or any personal belongings.

There I continued to receive and distribute Bibles. I lived at the church for seven years. And how can I tell of the joy I had there with the Lord? I can say with the psalmist: "Praise the LORD, all you servants of the LORD who minister by night in the house of the LORD" (Psalm 134:1).

But I didn't know that my dedication to the Lord there would stir all hell against me.

PART TWO

Chapter Eight

When Songs are Forbidden

S ing to the LORD a new song," says the Word of God in Psalm 96. But how do you sing a new song when songs are forbidden?

It was the winter of 1973. The country was still under the cruel dictatorship of Nicolae Ceauşescu. Christians were persecuted in all sorts of ways and controlled even in what they sang.

The church continued to be my place of refuge. As long as I was there I felt safe. But outside in the street the police were still trying to find a reason to arrest me. That is why I lived there in semi-hiding.

It was a cold day at the beginning of December and I was making the fire in the stove. It took a lot of wood to heat the one-room building with its six drafty windows and old door. There were ten long wooden benches on each side of the aisle; in front was the communion table, and behind it the pulpit; to the right was an old pump organ, and to the left were rows of chairs. Behind the pulpit, a long, thick velvet curtain separated the church from the woodshed. All around the church was a fence with a heavy gate, which I was careful to lock every evening.

There was a knock at the door and a lady came in. She was the wife of one of the preachers.

"Hello, Genovieva," she said, giving me a hug, "how about your getting the children together and preparing a Christmas program? You could teach them some songs and have them recite Scriptures. They could come for a practice every day now that they are on vacation. Sister Maria is already preparing Christmas boxes, and as usual the children are getting very excited."

"I'd be glad to," I said.

"I will get the children to come tomorrow at four," she offered.

"I would like new songs with joyful tunes. Where can I find such songs?" I asked her.

"There are none in our country. I'm afraid you will have to make do with old ones. Christian composers who dared to write songs for God have been put in prison."

Only then did I realize that there were so few children's Christmas songs in Romania.

I wanted so much to praise God with new melodies, and my need for songs was very urgent. I knew that the Christmas program had to be very special. There were only sixteen days until Christmas. The children were going to come the next day and I didn't have any songs.

Now it was night and I was all by myself in the church hall. The curtains were drawn, and the lights were off, but the fire was still burning. Behind the pulpit there was plenty of room for me to read my Bible by the light of a candle, to pray, and to sleep. But this night there was no time to sleep. I was struggling with the Lord on my knees, "Lord, please give me songs. The children are coming at four o'clock tomorrow afternoon."

Suddenly a tune came to my mind and I found myself humming it. It was a lovely tune. *What tune is it?* I wondered. Ah, yes, I had learned it at school when I was twelve, an English traditional tune from my English textbook. Soon I found myself composing words to its joyful melody.

I had been good at composition in school, but never until then had I used this gift for God. I worked until late that night at the first stanza and refrain until there was rich imagery, rhyme, and rhythm, and so that the accents came in the right places. There came a point when I knew it was ready:

> It is snowing outside
> With big snowflakes;
> Everywhere is beautiful:
> The gardens have put on
> Their whitest garments.
> And as I watch the snowflakes

Floating gently in the air,
I am happy that through Jesus
I am as white as snow.
Like a snowflake,
Like a snowflake,
Through Him I want to be;
A snow star,
A little white star
Shining for Him
Day and night.

Then I wrote the second stanza with the same care. I imagined the children dressed in blue blouses; and a little girl, dressed as a snowflake, as the soloist. I also imagined the choir swinging toward the right in the rhythm of the music, and the little girl dressed as the snowflake swinging toward the left in a dance. My father would play the violin, Teodor would be at the pump organ, and my friend Silvia would play the guitar.

The next day ten children came for the practice. They were boys and girls aged six to twelve. We practiced the new song dozens of times that afternoon until it sounded perfect. The instruments blended in beautifully.

"I love that song, Genovieva," said Petru.

"I'd so much like to be the snowflake," said Ligia with a wistful expression.

I didn't know it then, but this song would remain a favorite for the generations to come, and every year a little child would dream of being the snowflake.

"Can you teach us another song tomorrow?" asked six-year-old Gabi.

"Yes, I will," I said.

But in my heart I wondered where I was going to get another song!

After the children had gone home I cried to the Lord for help, *Lord give me more songs!*

Then the Lord brought to my mind that a team of Bible smugglers had brought my family a cassette of Christian songs. They had also left a radio-cassette player with it.

The next night again I did not sleep. Behind the pulpit I listened to the beautiful tunes. Some of them might have been Easter songs, but that night they all became Christmas carols: "For unto us a Child is Born," "Mary Knocked from House to House," "One Evening in the Fields," "Three Shepherds," and "It is Night and Everyone is Sleeping."

But my joy was soon to be threatened. The next afternoon the pastor came to the church with bad news.

"I have to inform the church that we are not allowed to sing unauthorized songs anymore," he said. "They all need to be approved by the government. We are even supposed to use this revised edition of the hymn book," he said, handing me a copy.

I looked through it, and my eyes stopped at a well-known Christmas carol.

"So instead of 'Jesus Christ, King of kings' they want us to sing, 'Jesus Christ, King of believers' and instead of 'every knee shall bow to the newborn King' they want us to sing 'every believer will kneel down....' Who made these changes?" I asked the pastor, astonished.

"Petru Popa, a poet from Ploieşti," he said. "I knew him personally. But the day he finished the job he was struck dead by an unseen hand."

"Then God can protect the songs," I said, "because it is He who commanded us to praise Him."

"They want to control those who write songs," the pastor said. "Traian Dorz and Nicolae Moldovanu are already in prison, and they will be there for many years."

Suddenly I realized the need to hide the fact that I was composing new songs. I needed not only new songs, but also wisdom from God.

The ten children came every day for practices for the Christmas program, as did the instrumentalists. The day finally arrived, and the church was overcrowded with some three hundred people crammed into the small building. The choir was set up to the right of the pulpit and the children were dressed in blue. Gabi, the soloist, was dressed all in white with a white ribbon in her hair. Next to the choir was the orchestra, and behind it was the Christmas tree, as high as the ceiling and richly decorated with silver balls and bells and snow stars.

The Christmas program was a great success. My dream had come true.

"You should repeat the program next Sunday," the pastor said at the end of the evening.

"And keep the choir going," his wife added.

"I liked how the children were swaying from side to side," someone remarked.

"Can I join the choir too?" other children asked.

"You can all come," I said. "We will have practices every Sunday afternoon."

This is how the children's choir in Iași started. I called it the Sion Choir, and it grew to sixty children. More children came, but we didn't have enough seats for them. How many adventures and risks were ahead of us, and how many blessings too! People were going to come from all over the country to hear the choir, and we were going to travel all over Romania to sing in churches.

The need for new songs remained. As I was praying for more tunes, the Lord brought to my mind the radio that we had received with the cassette recorder. It was forbidden to listen to shortwave radio, but the curtains were drawn and I kept the volume very low while searching for stations. There behind the pulpit I found a new source of songs: Christian broadcasts in several languages. When I found a nice tune I recorded it, then worked through the night to make up the words. This is why the Sion Choir had such a variety of beautiful tunes, and in the next few years had a repertoire of well over a hundred songs. Our songs came from England, France, Italy, Greece, Israel, Switzerland, from Africa and America, from Australia and New Zealand.

Sometimes, though, I couldn't get any tunes for weeks. Either there were no suitable songs or the broadcasts were jammed. Twice I used the signature tunes at the beginning of programs. One of them, from Israel, is still a favorite: "Where can I Go from You, Lord?"

I learned that nobody could stop us from praising God, even in the hardest of times. I didn't know at that time that the Sion Choir was going to be used by God to inspire many thousands of children to sing for Him in times of persecution.

Chapter Nine

The Telephone Call

It was in the summer of 1975 that our children's choir was invited for the first time to travel and sing away from home. A children's choir traveling and singing to God was unheard of at that time of persecution in Romania. *Will the secret police close their eyes or will they stop us?* I wondered. We had to trust God and be ready at the same time to pay the price for showing our faith in Him.

After a train journey of six hours, we arrived in Bucharest at noon. The streets of the capital city were crowded, and the forty children walked two by two holding hands, so as not to get lost. Daniel led the way; Silvia, Teodor, and Nelu walked with the children; and I came last, holding two of the youngest ones by their hands. Daniel was a young seminarian who lived in Bucharest, and he had planned this trip for us. We were to sleep at the Baptist Seminary on Strada Berzei, which was within walking distance of the railway station. We were to sing in four churches in the city.

The seminary was an old, two-floor stone building surrounded by a paved yard and a fence covered with pink climbing roses. In the middle of the yard was a statue of a man sowing seed, and at the back was a water fountain. The building consisted of classrooms, guest rooms, dormitories, a canteen, and a gymnasium.

"Welcome!" said sister Bărbătei. "I heard a lot about you and the children, and we cannot wait to hear you sing. Now I will lead you straight to your place."

The forty children quietly followed her through the hall into the gymnasium. There were mattresses laid all over the floor, and soon each child had chosen one.

"It is so much fun to sleep all in the same room," said eight-year-old Gabriela.

"And we can have a pillow fight," said Cornel.

"Be sure to come to the dining room at five o'clock for soup and apple pie," our hostess added.

"Let's pray," I said, "and thank the Lord for this place and ask Him to use us for His glory this evening."

One after the other, the children thanked the Lord for the trip and asked for His blessing.

Just then, a middle-aged couple appeared at the door. I recognized them as Mr. and Mrs. Lupu and went out into the hall to talk to them.

"The police are here," Mrs. Lupu said. She was a tall, elegant lady with a fresh hairdo. She and her husband were in charge of the building, and they lived in one of the apartments there. They were also informers for the secret police.

"They want to see the identity cards of the adults accompanying the choir," Mr. Lupu explained. He was small and fat, with a long pointed nose and thick brown oily hair, combed backward.

I went back into the dormitory to get my purse. My heart was beating fast and I could sense danger.

I had come to this same place the year before. Young people from Christian families all over the country who sought entrance to college in Bucharest came here for free accommodation. I had wanted to try to enter the university in Bucharest, with the hope that they didn't know who I was. As I needed a place to sleep for one week, I went to stay there with several other girls.

One afternoon as I entered the yard, this same couple met me, asked me for my identity card, and disappeared with it into another room.

"You can't stay here," Mrs. Lupu had said when she returned. "The secret police say you are dangerous."

"What did I do?" I asked.

"We don't know. They say you are an enemy of the country, and that you should leave this place immediately."

"Please, let me stay until I finish my entrance exams. I don't have money for a hotel. I don't have any friends here either," I pleaded.

"Get out of here!" they both shouted. "We don't want to bring trouble on the seminary."

"But my father is a preacher," I said. "We send tithes from our church here."

"Out!" the man shouted and spat in my face.

I went to the water fountain there in the yard to wash my face. There I heard the Lord speaking to my heart: *Remember that they spat on Me too*. And the presence of the Lord filled my heart with peace.

Now, this year, the scene was a similar one. There was silence now in the hall where a police officer was standing, looking at the five adults' papers. After checking the name and the face, he gave them back. Then he came to me.

"Everyone is allowed to stay here except you, Miss Genovieva Sfatcu. You have to leave."

"Leave? I am the leader of the choir. We are expected to sing in churches. We cannot be separated."

Little by little, I started to understand that I was illegal wherever I was, and the reason was simply that I served the Lord.

"We will find a solution," Daniel intervened. "I am responsible for their coming here. She has to stay with the children. We will find another place for all of them, maybe...."

The policeman left. The children ate in silence. That Wednesday evening hundreds of people came to hear the choir in the church on Strada Basarab. However, there was tension in the air. The place was thick with secret police. The children took their seats on the platform. They were dressed in mauve and pink blouses. Teodor took his place at the organ, and Silvia and Nelu were ready with their guitars. Daniel took his place at the pulpit alongside the two pastors. I led the choir with some apprehension. After the children's first songs, the pastors smiled and even laughed with delight. They even asked us to repeat certain songs. As the children sang praises to the Lord, the power of God fell upon the whole congregation and many started to cry. A sister overheard a conversation between two agents.

"I can't stop them," one of them said.

"Neither can I," came the whispered reply.

The Lord was there with us. We sang many songs as usual, and the children recited Scriptures in between. Many recorded our songs on tape.

That evening we walked back to the seminary.

"I don't see where else you could go with so many children," Daniel said. "You have to stay here, I'm afraid."

"Let's pray, children, that the police don't come back," I said.

The Lord heard our prayers and the police never returned.

The next days we were occupied with long hours of recording sessions that were held in two churches. Different brothers came to record the choir. If a child coughed or dropped a pen on the floor, we had to start the recording all over again.

On Saturday we sang in the church on Strada Popa Rusu. We walked there two hours ahead of time to pray and to practice for the program. It was a very hot day. Pastor Sărac received us very well and gave each of the children a bottle of ice-cold Pepsi, which they never forgot. They were so happy!

Long before the program started, the church filled to capacity. Hundreds of people were crowded inside, standing in every corner, even around the pulpit. They all came to hear the Sion Children's Choir.

"Don't forget," I reminded the children, "that you are not allowed to look at the audience while singing. Look at me for any signal and pray all the time between songs. Pray also for Cornelia, the soloist, to sing well."

"We will, we will," the children assured me.

The program was a success and many recorded that evening of praise. At the end, everyone wanted to give the children a hug and to wish them God's blessing. Sisters prepared sandwiches, vanilla cookies, and cheese pies.

"It is Cornelia's birthday," a little boy remarked. "She is nine."

"Then we need to get her a gift," the elders responded. "She sang so beautifully that she stole everyone's heart."

The elders came back with a doll and presented it to her with a bouquet of red roses.

"The doll is bigger than Cornelia," the children said and they laughed.

"We want to make a choir like yours," the elders said.

On the way back to the seminary that evening, I thought the trouble was over. When we arrived, Mr. Lupu met us in the hall.

"You won't come to my church with the choir," he said, shaking his finger. "No way! The secret police said so."

"But the church is expecting us," I said.

"Your stay here is over, and I advise you all to go to the railway station and catch the night train home. Leave right now!"

"But tomorrow is Sunday and another church is expecting us," I tried to explain. "Besides, I cannot change the train tickets."

But he had turned and disappeared into his apartment.

"We need to pray, children," I said before we went to sleep that night. "Mr. Lupu is trying all he can to scare us away. He has just told us to go home."

The lights were dim in the gymnasium where we were. The children, dressed in their pajamas, knelt down on the floor to pray. *There is no salvation for us but God*, I thought. *Is Mr. Lupu going to call the police?*

One after another, the children prayed in their own words: "Lord, You know that the church is expecting us. Please change Mr. Lupu's heart."

And another one prayed: "Lord, please help us to finish our trip."

After all the children had prayed, it became silent. I turned the lights off and I continued to pray as Psalm 50:15 says: "Call upon me in the day of trouble; I will deliver you, and you will honor me."

Just then the telephone rang in the hall. It was a long-distance call for Mr. Lupu.

"What?" we heard his scared voice say. "She is dead? How can that be? I have to come? I guess I have to. There is a train at midnight. We'll get dressed and we will be there in the morning."

We watched through the window as Mr. and Mrs. Lupu left for an unexpected funeral in their family.

"You can come!" the elders told us next morning. "He is gone. Everyone wants you there."

"Hurrah!" the children shouted and clapped their hands.

On Sunday morning, we sang in the Baptist Church on 23 August Boulevard. All went very well. In the evening, we sang in the church on Calea Ferentari as planned. It was very crowded, and even the yard was full of people. The Lord used us once again, and we learned that it is never too late to call upon the Lord. He would deliver us again and again, and we would glorify Him in more and more difficult situations.

Chapter Ten

Christmas under Persecution

Christmas is a time when we owe God thanks for the greatest gift He ever gave us: Jesus Christ our Savior. But the enemy will always do his best to spoil our joy at this season. In Romania, the communists tried year after year to stop this celebration, and President Ceaușescu had his mind set on making Christmas illegal.

It was December 20, 1975. I was twenty-four years old, still living by myself at the church. During the day I would clean the building, and at night I slept there in semi-hiding.

Everything is so beautiful, I thought. *The fire burning in the stove and the lights on the Christmas tree....* From the piano to the lower branches of the fir tree there were two long poles, supported by wooden stands. On them I hung about 150 baskets with gifts I had made by hand with help from my brother Teodor and the girl who played the guitar with the choir, Silvia. We made these baskets by cutting the parts out of cardboard, then sewing them together and covering them with red, green, and blue crepe paper. I then filled them with candies, cookies, and nuts and worked hard to give joy to all the children who would come. The children's choir I was leading had also worked hard to learn the ten Christmas carols.

All of a sudden there was a knock at the door. I went to open it and there stood Mr. Andronic, the Inspector of Religion for the county of Iași. He took a look inside the church and then, without taking his hands out of his black leather coat pockets, said angrily, "I came to tell you again, Miss

Genovieva, as I told your father and the pastor: Get that Christmas tree out of the church!"

He was small and skinny, in his late fifties, and always wore dark glasses and a hat.

"It attracts too many children to the church," he added. "The government is the only authority allowed to educate children in our country."

He always likes to threaten us, I thought, watching him disappear down the street.

I remembered when I was a little girl. I could not wait for Christmas to come. I would gaze at the decorations, and I liked it when sister Maria put off all the lights and lit the candles on the Christmas tree. Then we would all sing "Silent Night." After that she would give us each a basket full of gifts. There would be a piece of Turkish delight, several fondant candies wrapped in foil, a vanilla cookie, a nut, and a tangerine.

It was hard to find sweets in the shops at Christmastime. Fir trees and candles appeared just before New Year's Eve. The same was true for flour, vanilla, and yeast, which we used for baking.

One year the secret police arrested many teenagers as they were coming home from Christmas programs at church. They were taken to the police station and beaten. Another time, while we were Christmas caroling, they followed us with police dogs. I wondered what they were going to do this year.

Many thoughts crossed my mind. Last Sunday, Pastor Radu had read from the Bible: "Blessed are those who wash their robes, that they may have the right to the tree of life and may go through the gates into the city" (Revelation 22:14).

After the service, my aunt shared with me a dream. "I dreamed of a beautiful sunset," she said. "What could it mean?"

The pastor's wife came to me too. "I dreamed that a snake bit my husband on his right temple," she said. "Pray for us!"

Later on the same day, old sister Boca also shared with me, "I had a strange dream. We were in the church. There were three chairs behind the pulpit and the one in the middle was hit by an unseen hand. It broke in pieces and fell to the floor."

Two days passed. It was now December 22, about eight o'clock in the morning. The church gate and door were locked. I had had a late night and was still sleeping on a bench with my clothes and boots on. Suddenly I heard a loud knock at the gate.

Someone shouted, "Hello! Hello!"

I went outside. It was a policeman and he started to speak from behind the fence.

"Do you know someone by the name of Radu Cruceru?" he asked.

"Of course. He is our pastor."

"He was found dead in the forest near the village of Scânteia. His body is at the morgue and we found this address on his papers. I want you to tell his family and friends," he muttered before leaving in a hurry.

I ran home as fast as I could. My family was the first to see the pastor as he lay on that cold marble bed. He had a wound on his right temple, and though dead, he was heavily guarded by secret police.

Pastor Radu's body was brought into the church for the viewing. His clothes were put in the woodshed behind the church. My father and brothers Teodor and Costică put on plastic gloves and examined the clothes and shoes.

"The clothes are full of blood on the right side," my father said, "and the blood went into his right shoe. It seems that he was beaten while standing up, or else he stood up after being hit. On the judgment day his blood will be avenged."

Then my father wrote a report about his death. "Hide it," he said to me. I hid the report with the archives of the church.

On December 24, the pastor's body was transported to another town for the funeral. Many from the church went along to comfort his wife.

This murder was very well planned to spoil our Christmas, I thought. *So much preparation, and now all seems to have been in vain.*

"You should take the Christmas tree and throw it in the back garden," brother Ion suggested to me. "It is now a time of mourning."

But I was uncomfortable with his suggestion. This man was an informer for the secret police. He would stand up uninvited in church and pray something like this: "Thank You, Lord, for the beautiful freedom we have in our country."

"I will see about that," I said. "I will have to talk with my father. Now that the pastor is dead, my father is the one responsible."

Suddenly I knew I could not allow the children to be disappointed, and I remembered a Scripture: "Do not be afraid. I bring you good news of great joy that will be for all the people. Today in the town of David a Savior has been born to you; he is Christ the Lord" (Luke 2:10–11).

Quickly I aired the church, washed the floors, and shook the carpets outside in the snow. I dusted the pews and brought branches of fir tree in from the garden. I made the fire in the stove and lit the candles in the windows. I put on the Christmas lights around the pulpit and in the tree.

These policemen need to learn that nothing can stop us from giving glory to God for the birth of our Savior, I thought.

When five o'clock came the church was already full of people. The Sion Children's Choir took their seats up front. Dozens of other children came. Old Pastor Asiev, full of the Lord, went to the pulpit. He preached on the joy of Christmas. Then the organ and guitars started to play the first Christmas carol.

We celebrated with much joy that evening. I learned that if Satan tries to stop us from giving God the praise we owe at Christmastime, we shouldn't allow him to succeed. I told the children that nothing—neither trouble, nor persecution, nor death—can separate us from the love of Christ. And it was good that I told them these words, because soon they were going to be tested themselves.

Chapter Eleven

The Yellow Badge

One Sunday afternoon about half past three, I was in the church waiting for the children to come for choir practice, when Daniel rushed in.

"Genovieva," he said, gasping for breath. "My English teacher is in a tree, watching…two houses down the street. I think he took my number!"

Each schoolchild in Romania was required to wear a yellow badge on his left sleeve. On the badge was the child's number. In this way informers could easily trace them. Usually children would try to hide these badges, which were sewn on. But it was not always easy, especially if they had only one jacket, as was the case with Daniel.

The yellow armband sewn on his left sleeve read NR 875 / SC GEN 5. He was so faithful and so reliable, especially for a quiet boy of just twelve years, and I wished so much to come to his rescue.

First of all I went out to see for myself. On the left side of the street, in a garden full of roses, there was a marble monument on which was written, "In this house, in the year 1940, the first Communist Party meeting in Iași took place."

I gazed up into the cherry tree Daniel told me about, and I recognized my former university colleague, Ionescu, sitting hidden among the branches.

When I returned to the church I told Daniel, "He used to spy on me, too, when I was still at university. He will probably question you tomorrow"

"What shall I say?" Daniel asked, and his brown eyes showed concern.

"Remember the words of Jesus," I replied, holding his hand. "'When you are brought before…rulers and authorities, do not worry about how you will defend yourselves or what you will say, for the Holy Spirit will teach you at that time what you should say' (Luke 12:11–12)."

One after another, the children prayed for Daniel. "Lord, give him courage and wisdom tomorrow at school." Others prayed, "Lord, help Daniel to be a good witness for You."

On Monday morning, on his way to school, many questions passed through Daniel's mind. *Will I be able to be strong, like Daniel in the Bible? Will they put me in prison? Will I ever see my family and the choir again?* All he knew was that he was afraid.

Comrade Ionescu, his English teacher, came into the classroom, looking severe. He was small and skinny, with a pale face and blond hair combed over to one side. The class stood up to give the Pioneer salute.

"*Salut voios de Pionier!*" they said in unison, their right hands raised.

"*Salut voios,*" answered the teacher. "Sit down, please."

The sun was shining through the windows, but Daniel felt apprehensive. *Lord, help me!*

"Who has number 875?" the teacher asked from behind his desk.

Daniel stood up.

"Come up front."

Daniel walked slowly from the back of the classroom, trembling in his shoes.

"Tell us where you were yesterday," the teacher demanded.

"At church, Comrade Ionescu."

"Didn't you know that you were supposed to plant flowers in the communist cemetery?"

"On Sunday I go to church, Comrade. It is the Lord's Day."

"The Lord's Day? Are you a Christian?"

"Yes." Daniel nodded.

"Ha! Ha! Ha! Children, let's laugh together at him!"

Daniel looked at the teacher, then at the class. From everywhere he could hear "Ha! Ha! Ha!" Only a few were silent. Daniel felt as if his cheeks, ears, and nose were burning.

"What do you do at church? Do you pray to God?" Comrade Ionescu asked.

"Yes," Daniel answered, looking down.

"And how do you pray? Give us a demonstration."

Suddenly there was silence in the classroom.

Daniel closed his eyes, clasped his hands, raised his head, and prayed in a clear, loud voice. "Dear God, thank You that You gave Your Son, Jesus, to die for my sins. Thank You for saving me. Please bless Comrade Ionescu and my classmates and save them—"

"Stop! Stop! I forbid you to pray for us like that!"

Daniel stopped praying and opened his eyes.

"Either you must promise not to go to church anymore, or you will receive a punishment. Choose one or the other," Comrade Ionescu shouted.

Silence.

Lord, help me! Daniel prayed. *Promise that I will quit going to the church, and to the children's choir? No, I cannot do that.*

"All right.… So that all the students may learn what will happen if they go to church, go in that corner, kneel down, and keep your hands up until the end of the hour." Comrade Ionescu's face had purpled, and his jaw quivered in his rage at Daniel. "Keep your face to the wall."

Daniel went there and knelt with his hands up, face to the wall, as he was told. He did not want to cry, yet his eyes filled with tears. He felt humiliated and he thought that all his classmates would be scared of Jesus forever. The first five minutes were not too hard. But then it became harder and harder. He looked at the clock on the wall. *Five more minutes! Lord, help me!*

Finally the bell rang and the class was dismissed. But, to his surprise, some of his classmates looked at him with sympathy.

"You did great!" one boy whispered as he passed. "I want to ask you some questions about your faith, when nobody sees us."

"I would like to go with you to church next Sunday," another classmate said.

Later on there were other questions about Jesus and about how to be saved. Daniel was glad to answer them.

When he went home that day, he hardly had the strength to hold his bag, but inside he was happy.

One week later Daniel was proud to share with the choir how the Lord had helped him. And for now he was glad to be out of his teacher's hands.

Chapter Twelve

The Red Umbrella

It was a rainy Sunday afternoon in the autumn. The blocks of flats in the Socola district of Iași on the Bahlui River looked a dismal gray. There, in a flat on the first floor, lived Otilia, one of the first members in the choir. She was a fourteen-year-old now with rosy cheeks, blue eyes, and long, brown shoulder-length hair parted in the middle. The flat was nicely furnished. Otilia was dressed for church in a navy blue suit that her mother had made.

"You can't go to church," her father said. He was a tall man with neatly combed hair, and a nervous tic that made him blink all the time.

"Please, let me go," Otilia answered in her low, warm voice. "Ella is waiting for me in the hall."

"Don't you see, it's pouring rain?" her father insisted.

"That's all right," Otilia answered, looking straight at her father. *You'd always stop me from going if you could*, she thought.

"Listen, take my red umbrella," said Otilia's mother, a fat woman with her hair in a bun.

"But don't lose it," her father warned. "It is brand new, and it cost your mother four days' wages. Don't you dare come home without it!"

Lord, help me not to lose it! she prayed as she went out the door. She thought how generous it was of her mother to lend it to her.

The tram took Otilia and Ella to the center of the city in ten minutes. From the tram stop it was half a mile on foot.

"My father does not believe in God," Otilia said. "He works for the secret police."

"What about your mother?" asked Ella. She was the daughter of one of the preachers in the church.

"My mother is a Christian," Otilia answered. "She goes to the Pentecostal Church on Strada Anton Panu. I go to your church because I like to sing in the children's choir. But my father picks on the smallest things to stop us going to church. Since I became a Christian two years ago, it seems as though everything has gone against me. I have been persecuted both at school and at home."

"We must pray for your father," Ella answered. "God answered so many prayers when we prayed with the children's choir."

"Yes, we prayed for money for the trip and it came.... We prayed for shoes and clothes and the Lord sent them.... We prayed for food for Ionel's family, and they received it.... We prayed that the secret police would be blinded when we received New Testaments, and they never saw anything. But I'd like to know if God answers *my* prayers."

"I'm sure He will," Ella answered as they were approaching the church.

The choir practice started soon after they arrived at the church, and it went on for an hour and a half. The church service then followed, from six to eight. The hall was packed, and many came just to hear the children sing. The choir sang six or seven songs, accompanied by the organ and guitars. Neighbors who were afraid to come in opened their windows so that they too could hear them. Otilia recited a poem, which she had learned by heart.

When the service was over, she hurried out.

She sat down on a bench to wait for the tram. The rain had stopped so she leaned the umbrella against the wall. She looked at the lighted shop window of the store across the road, but her thoughts were far away. *Why don't I have a father like Ella's? Life would be so much easier.* Soon the tram came and Otilia jumped on.

She arrived at her apartment and was about to ring the bell, when she suddenly remembered.

The umbrella!

She ran back to the tram stop and boarded the next tram for town. *I left it leaning up against the wall. What if someone took it? Lord, keep it for me! I can't face my father without it, and my mother will be upset too.* She got off in the center and looked beside the bench where she had sat down. The umbrella was nowhere to be seen. *Oh, Lord! What shall I do?* Tears rolled down her cheeks.

Otilia crossed the street to the store, which was still open.

"Did you see a red umbrella?" she asked the lady at the counter. "I left it at the tram stop."

"A red umbrella?" The lady's face lit up. "Yes, someone just brought it in a few minutes ago. Here you are."

"Thank you *very* much, I'm so thankful," she said, taking the umbrella.

Half an hour later she was home and returned the umbrella to her mother. There was the smell of baked bread in the kitchen, and she was so happy.

The sky had cleared now and from her bedroom window she could see the stars. *Now I know for sure that God hears my prayers!*

Otilia would need this assurance in the days to come.

Chapter Thirteen

Iulian, the Gypsy Boy

Iulian was a gypsy boy of twelve with long, curly hair and dark eyes. His smile showed two large front teeth. Dressed in an old corduroy suit, he wore what seemed to be his father's boots. Nobody paid him any attention until he became a Christian and joined the children's choir. After that he became a real threat to the secret police.

Iulian became a good friend of mine. He helped me clean the church, and I in return taught him to read and write, using the New Testament as the textbook. It was not easy to teach him to read, especially since he had a tendency to add extra sounds at the end of words, as gypsies often do.

After many days of hard work, I knew that he had gotten it. Little did I know that one day Iulian's ability to read would save my life.

The gypsy quarter, with its tents and horse-drawn caravans, was not far away from the church. It was evening and Iulian's family was sitting around the fire having supper.

"You can't go to church anymore," said his mother, while pouring boiling milk into the earthenware bowls. She was a big woman with a colorful, long dress and a scarf tied at the back of her head.

"I have to go, Mom," Iulian replied. "The choir is expecting me."

"It's very serious, boy," said his father, a short man with a moustache and a black hat. "The police even gave us money to keep you home."

"But Father"—Iulian squared his shoulders—"I have the time of my life when I go there, not like when I go to town. Children in town throw stones at me and call me names. The other day the baker pushed me out of his store and kicked me. I swear I will never go into that store again. But at the church they love me. The children let me sit next to them. Pastor Radu prayed for me by name one Sunday evening."

"Iulian, it's very dangerous," his father said. "We have been reported to the secret police. We will be put in prison if we are not careful."

"They said," continued Iulian's mother, "that the pastor pronounced a blessing over you. The police called it a curse. They said he prayed, 'May this boy become a preacher for the gypsies.' They didn't like that at all."

"Yes, yes, that's right," his father said, crossing his arms. "They said that should never happen. They don't want a gypsy church."

"They also want to put Genovieva, the choir director, on trial. They set it all up, and you are going to be a witness," said Iulian's mother. "They said she should have sent you to school instead of letting you help her clean the church."

Iulian forgot about the boiled milk and corn mush in his bowl. His younger brother and sister were eating while watching with big eyes.

That evening Iulian went to bed early, but he couldn't fall asleep. He thought of Pastor Radu, who had prayed for him and who had been murdered since that time. He had seen with his own eyes his bloodstained clothes in the woodshed at the church. *Will they kill me too?* he thought.

Late at night, when everybody was asleep, Iulian sneaked out of the door and ran as fast as he could to the church where I was living. He jumped over the high fence and knocked at the window.

"Genovieva, it's me, Iulian."

"Come around the back," I answered.

"Genovieva," Iulian said, "I have to speak with you. The police are after us. They have witnesses. Two neighbors wrote declarations that they saw me coming to church instead of going to school. They say you took me away from school! But you never did that. I don't want you to go to prison because of me."

"Iulian, do not be afraid. You have been such a good friend to me in the last two years. I am ready to suffer for you, for Christ's sake."

"They try to stop me coming to the choir too. That would be hard on me."

"We will pray, Iulian. And don't forget that nothing can separate us from the love of Christ. God is so strong that our enemies are like dwarfs in front of Him. When you are called to the police, don't forget that the

Lord will go with you. He will teach you what to answer. Now go, before anybody sees us."

The next day all the family was summoned to the police station. There, in a room filled with powerful communists, Iulian saw his parents give declarations in fear. The two neighbors were there too, brought in as witnesses.

"What did you do at the church during the week, Iulian?" asked Andronic, the inspector of churches.

"I watered the garden, dusted the pews, sang songs, and read stories from the Bible.… I love Genovieva more than my grandmother, sir!"

"That girl has interrupted your schooling," the inspector replied. A smirk crept over his face. "Any person who causes a child to miss school should be punished. It is illegal to be illiterate in Romania. So, a boy of twelve like you cannot read or write because of her."

"But sir," said Iulian, standing up, "I never went to school in my life! Boys there hate us gypsies. I swear I would never go. But I *can* read and write. Genovieva taught me. Let me show you."

Taking out a worn-out New Testament from his pocket he opened and read, "'For God so loved the world that he gave his one and only Son, that whoever believes in him shall not perish but have eternal life.'"

"That's enough," said the policeman, embarrassed. "I didn't know you could read."

Iulian's parents looked at each other in amazement. Suddenly they became so proud of their son. But the witnesses were ashamed.

"You are all dismissed now," said Andronic.

Another day passed, and when evening came, Iulian was reading from the New Testament to the gypsies around the fire. They were listening to words they had never heard before.

"Jesus said, 'I am the gate; whoever enters through me will be saved. He will come in and go out, and find pasture. The thief comes only to steal and kill and destroy; I have come that they may have life, and have it to the full. I am the good shepherd. The good shepherd lays down his life for the sheep'" (John 10:9–11).

As he read these verses, Iulian wondered: *Am I ready to suffer for the Lord?*

Chapter Fourteen

The Recording Session

One Sunday afternoon I was with the children's choir in the church, practicing for the evening program. Listening to Christian radio broadcasts was forbidden. Doing recordings for a Christian radio station was a crime. But the government claimed Romania had religious freedom, and so police would not come *inside* a church building.

"We came to record the choir," said two visitors as they entered the church. "We heard that they sing so beautifully."

I remembered how I used to draw the curtains, put off the lights, lock the doors, and tune in to a shortwave broadcast. I was so encouraged by the messages and the Christian music coming from far away. The desire to do a recording that would bless others overcame my fear, and I was ready to take the risk.

"Yes," I said. "We are just having a practice. Come on in! I hope nobody followed you."

"Hello, Genovieva, I am Nelu," said a tall, young man as he shook hands with me.

"And I'm Mitică," said the other man, who was older.

"Welcome. I'm glad you made it. Have a seat."

"We have the recording equipment in the car. Is it all right to bring it in?" Nelu whispered.

"Yes, bring it in," I said. "But make sure no one sees you."

"This recording has to be very clear. As you know, it is for shortwave radio," Mitică explained discreetly.

"We will try our best. We're ready to start as soon as you have set up the equipment. The children are still on vacation and they can stay till late."

Soon the reel-to-reel recorders and microphones were set up.

"Let's start with 'My Harp will Play for You,' then we will try 'The Law of the Lord,'" I told the children.

The first song went well and the radio men seemed pleased.

Boom! Boom! Boom! Boom!

The choir stopped abruptly. It sounded like there had been an explosion on the street.

I went to the window. "It is a big truck stopped in front of the church," I said.

All sorts of revving noises could be heard from the engine for the next ten minutes.

"This is what the secret police often do when we have special services," Teodor explained. "We must wait until they are gone."

"The truck is leaving now. Let's try the second song again," I said.

The recording went well this time.

"Now let's try 'All is New in my Heart.'…"

Boom! Boom! Boom! Boom!

"That sounds like exhaust backfiring," said Teodor, jumping up and looking through the window. "It is another truck."

"We had better take a break, children," I said. "Our visitors brought you some candies."

"Thank you!" the children said, passing a large bag of milk candies around.

"Let's try 'All is New in my Heart' again," I said as the noise stopped. "Also 'I Delight to Do Your Will.'"

Boom! Boom! Boom! Boom! came from in front of the church as we started the second song.

"We'll have to stop again," I said. "Everyone pray after me: Father, help us to finish this recording for Your glory. These brothers came from far away to record our choir. In Jesus' name we pray. Amen."

Boom! Boom! Boom! Boom! All sorts of deafening noises filled the street and the church.

"It is another big truck," I said, looking through the window. "They are committed to hinder the recording."

"I have an idea," said Teodor. "Let's go to the Pentecostal Church. I often go there to play the organ. The road is narrow and it is a dead end. The trucks wouldn't be able to get down there."

"Let's go, children," I said.

"Yeah, let's go!" the children chorused.

In a matter of minutes, the equipment was packed up and the forty children were walking out of the church. As they passed the truck they waved mischievously at the driver.

"I hope you will be able to repair your truck," Petrică shouted.

Within half an hour, the choir was in the Pentecostal Church building. Recorders and microphones were soon set up, and Teodor was happy to play the organ, which was better than the pump organ in the Baptist Church.

"We have only recorded three songs. Let's try to do another three for now," I said, "'It's as Simple as ABC,' 'If it Weren't for Jesus' and 'On Untrodden Paths.'"

The children sang beautifully, and the two radio men carefully monitored the recording levels.

"That's wonderful," they said after they had finished. "Choose some more, Genovieva. Quickly, before something else happens."

"'We are One in the Lord,' 'Your Loving-Kindness,' 'Jesus is Wonderful,' and if you have the strength, 'Jericho' and 'Jacob's Ladder,'" I ordered.

The children sang with smiling faces. Nelu and Mitică, the recording technicians, smiled back at them all the time. But while they were on the second verse of "Jericho," we were suddenly interrupted.

Vrrrmm! Vrrrmm! Vrrrmm! Vrrrmm!

What's that? I wondered.

I went outside to look. Teodor followed.

"Secret policemen on motorcycles…. They are going up and down the street. We have to pray again."

All the children followed me in a prayer, "Lord, You delivered us from the trucks. Please deliver us from the motorcycles!"

Vrrrmm! Vrrrmm! Vrrrmm! Vrrrmm!

"There are at least four motorcyclists in black leather suits," said Teodor. "They come and go."

"At least the trucks gave us a break from time to time and we could record songs in between," said Cătălin. "But these motorcycles don't stop at all."

Vrrrmm! Vrrrmm! Vrrrmm! Vrrrmm! rattled our eardrums for the next ten minutes.

I prayed again with the children.

A moment later, someone began screaming outside. We dashed to the windows.

"Get away from here," a woman was shouting from her yard at the motorcyclists. "I have a sick child in the house."

"Couldn't you find anywhere else to play?" shouted an old man, picking up a brick to throw at them.

"Get away from our street," other neighbors shouted, shaking their fists.

Soon after that the motorcyclists left. There was silence in the street. The children sang fifteen more songs, and the recordings came out beautifully.

"They will try to steal your tapes," I said to the radio men while they were packing up. "You must be very careful."

"Everything is arranged," said Nelu. "Someone else will get them out of the country for us." Then they packed up their equipment, said good-bye to the children, and left.

A month passed, and brother Pricop, one of the elders, came to the church very excited. "I heard the Sion Children's Choir on shortwave radio last night. It sounded wonderful!"

"The Lord always blesses us when we have the courage to follow Him," I told the choir. The children shouted for joy.

And because we followed the Lord, our songs were copied on thousands of cassettes and broadcast many times all over the country into many homes.

Chapter Fifteen

The Three Coats

It was a cold day in early December, and the Christmas holidays were fast approaching. Inside the church on Strada Sărărie a warm fire burned in the stove. The children's choir was at the regular Sunday afternoon practice, and the children were busy talking about the trip ahead of them. They had been invited to sing in churches in Cluj, Oradea, and Arad, towns three hundred miles away. The churches in that area had paid for the train tickets.

"We will travel for one day and one night by train," said Tatiana.

"We will sleep on the train," said Nelu. "It will be great fun!"

"My mother is making *cozonac* with Turkish delight for me," said Laura. "I will take some for the trip."

In the third row of the children's choir, Cornelia, their soloist, didn't show any excitement. Neither did Miceta, her sister, who sat next to her. Gabriela, in the last row, was also sad, and looking down.

"Why are you so sad?" I asked them.

"Genovieva, we don't have coats," answered Cornelia. "Neither me nor Miceta. But we want to go on the trip so much!"

"And my coat is full of patches. I am ashamed to go with it," added Gabriela.

The three girls started to cry. A coat was very expensive. A Christian had to work at least two weeks in order to buy one.

"Can anybody help?" I asked the choir. "We cannot go without them. It would be so sad to leave them behind!"

"My mother cut up the blanket on our bed and made me a coat out of it," said Lidia, who had many brothers and sisters.

"And I share the same coat with my brother," added Beni. "He goes to school in the morning and I go in the afternoon."

"I can see that nobody has a spare coat. There is only one thing we can do," I said. "Let's pray and ask God to help us."

I knelt down and so did all fifty children. One by one each child prayed, "Dear God, please send three coats for Cornelia, Miceta, and Gabriela. We want them to come with us on the trip."

Several days passed. The girls still had no coats.

There were only seven more days before the day of departure. We had choir practice almost every day.

"Has Jesus sent the coats yet?" eight-year-old Laura asked me one day.

"Not yet," I replied.

"But will He send them in time?" an older boy asked.

"Yes," I answered. "He is never late."

Two days before we were due to leave, the postman brought a notification for me. A parcel had arrived at the central post office. I quickly went to pick it up. It was quite big, but not too heavy. *Whatever could it be?* I thought.

When the children were gathered for the final rehearsal, I brought in the parcel.

"We received this in the mail," I told the children. "It is addressed to the children's choir."

The children stared with curiosity at the parcel. It was postmarked Oradea.

I cut the string and peeled off the tape. All the children watched in silence. Inside was a note that read: "From Christians in Holland who heard about your beautiful choir."

The first item I pulled out was a blue coat made of nice soft, thick wool with big buttons.

"Cornelia, try it on!" She had blue eyes.

The second item was a green coat, brand new, with red lining.

"Miceta, this is for you!"

The third was a warm, brown coat with a white fur collar. It seemed the right size for Gabriela.

"It's so nice," Cornelia said, "and fits me just right."

"Mine is wonderful!" said Miceta, feeling the wool texture of her new coat.

"I've never had such a beautiful coat in my life," said Gabriela.

All the children clapped and shouted for joy.

Then I knelt down and led them all in a prayer.

"Thank You, dear God, that You heard our prayers and sent a blue coat for Cornelia, to match her blue eyes; a green coat for Miceta, to match her green eyes; and a brown coat for Gabriela, to match her dark hair. Now they can go with us on the trip."

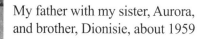

My father with my sister, Aurora, and brother, Dionisie, about 1959

My father at his office with the ladies who used to "steal" his potatoes, about 1963

Myself with Maria and Tolea Lazăr, and Mr. Balif, outside our home in Iaşi, March 1980

Doing my job at Iaşi Baptist Church, May 1978

My father (second from left, front), Pastor Radu Cruceru (center front), and the other elders of Iaşi Baptist Church, about 1974

The Sion Children's Choir in Iaşi Baptist Church, about 1977. My friend, Silvia, is playing the guitar and I am directing the choir

The Sion Children's Choir in the Baptist Church on Calea Ferentari, Bucharest, 1977

Directing the Sion Children's Choir in the
Baptist Church on Str. Basarab, Bucharest, 1977.
Teodor is playing the organ

The Sion Children's
Choir outside Pastor
Sărac's church on
Str. Popa Rusu,
Bucharest, 1975

The Sion Children's Choir outside the
church, March 1980. Carmen ("The Song
Book") is fifth from left in front row

Otilia
("The Red Umbrella"),
August 1986

Cornelia,
the choir's soloist
("The Temptation"),
May 1982

Children dressed in
Pioneers' uniforms
for Sunday activities

Below, Corina and
Iulian, August 1980

Above, Daniela
("The Parade"),
1983

Above, Mirela
("The Parade"),
April 1983

Corina (left), Mama, Laura, Iulian and Babi (front) in the kitchen of the family house ("The Hiding Place"), 1981

Laura and Babi, about 1981

Gabi ("A Kernel of Wheat"), about 1977

Corina and Iulian, February 1988

The Sion Children's Choir praying in the church, about 1977

Directing the Choir in the Baptist Church on Str. Basarab, Bucharest, 1978

The Sion Children's Choir outside Iaşi Baptist Church, March 1980.
I am in the front row (third from left) with my friends
Elena (second from left), and Silvia (fourth from right), and
brother, Teodor (third from right).

Chapter Sixteen

The Songbook

Carmen and Cătălin were new members in the children's choir. Carmen was eleven and her cousin, Cătălin, was a boy of twelve. Carmen was short, with wavy, light brown hair and blue eyes. Her cousin was a little taller, with brown eyes. Their parents were not Christians. One Sunday afternoon the cousins came to talk with me before the choir practice.

"Genovieva," Cătălin said, "we love the songs you teach us, but we don't know the words well enough. Don't you have a song book for us?"

"I don't have any," I replied. "We are not even allowed to have a typewriter. Silvia copies songs by hand for the children, but often it's too much for her."

"Why can't you copy them at a copying machine?" asked Carmen.

"The secret police guards such machines, to stop Christians from copying songs or portions of the Bible on them. To use a copying machine would be risky...but not impossible."

At that Carmen and Cătălin smiled at each other and left. Later they told me this story....

As it was the summer vacation, one evening they went to see their aunts, Ani and Luci. Arriving at the first floor of the block in Podu Roşu, the children rang the bell at apartment number three. The oak door opened.

"What a surprise! Come on in, dear children," said Aunt Luci. She was slender with blond hair that touched her shoulders.

"It's a joy to have you here," said Aunt Ani, taking their coats and hanging them on the coat stand. Ani and Luci were identical twins.

Carmen and Cătălin made themselves comfortable on the velvet sofa. Soon there were chocolate cakes and drinks on the table.

"Aunt Ani," Carmen began, eating her cake, "you and Aunt Luci once said you would do anything for us."

"Well, maybe I did," Aunt Ani answered from her plush green armchair. "We have no other nephew and niece, do we?"

"Besides, you are such lovely children," added Aunt Luci. "What is your request?"

"We need some songs copied for the choir," said Carmen.

"What choir?" Aunt Luci asked.

"The children's choir at church," Carmen said. "Since we have been living with Grandma, she takes us to church, and we joined the children's choir."

"We learned lots of songs, but the children never have enough song sheets," said Cătălin, between sips of lemonade. "Once you showed us the copying machine at the laboratory where you work."

"How many songs would need copying?" asked Aunt Luci.

"Well, we learned altogether seventy-eight songs," replied Carmen.

"And how many children are there?"

"About fifty," Carmen answered.

"Seventy-eight times fifty equals thirty-nine hundred," Aunt Ani calculated. "That's a lot of copies!"

"But you showed us that you just press a button and you can copy hundreds," said Cătălin.

"Are they typed?" asked Aunt Luci.

"No. Genovieva, our choir director, told us that Christians are not allowed to have a typewriter unless it's registered with the police," said Carmen.

"And they are not allowed to use a copying machine either," said Cătălin.

"Shhh! Don't speak so loud," whispered Aunt Ani.

There was silence for the next few minutes as Aunt Ani and Aunt Luci cleared the table. Then they went into the kitchen to speak privately. Carmen and Cătălin sat and waited in silence.

"We will help you," Aunt Ani said finally. "Be at the laboratory where we work at six o'clock tomorrow evening. You know your way there. But keep your mouths shut, or else we might end up in prison."

The Chemistry Department was in a vast stone structure with several floors and hundreds of rooms. At six o'clock sharp the next evening, Carmen and Cătălin entered the building and made their way to the laboratory on the third floor where their aunts worked. The students had gone home, and they were all by themselves now. A strong smell of chemicals met them as they walked past rows of test tubes and powders in all sorts of jars. Liquids bubbling through tubes made gurgling noises. At one end of the room stood a big copying machine and a typewriter.

"Did you bring the songs?" asked Aunt Ani, while Aunt Luci locked the doors from inside.

"Yes, here they are," said Carmen, handing her a stack of papers. "Seventy-eight handwritten songs."

"Let's get organized here," Aunt Luci said. "We cannot use the handwritten copies. It is too dangerous. I will type one song at a time, and Aunt Ani will get busy with the copying."

"Carmen, you watch the window for anything going on outside. And you, Cătălin, listen for noises in the hall," instructed Aunt Ani. "We should use a dim light. We don't want to be seen from outside."

For a while everything went smoothly. Aunt Luci typed one song at a time then handed it to Aunt Ani, who made fifty copies.

"There is a man walking up and down outside the building," Carmen said.

"Let me see," said Aunt Ani, going to the window and peeping out. "It is only the security guard. I don't think he will come inside."

Another hour of intense work passed.

"Let's have some coffee," Aunt Luci said. "It's nearly nine o'clock and I'm falling asleep at the typewriter."

The four of them had a few minutes' break and a cup of coffee. Soon they were back at work.

"A police car has stopped outside," Carmen announced in a scared voice from her position at the window. "The policeman is getting out of the car and speaking to the security guard. They are looking up. I think they saw me."

"Copier off!" Aunt Luci ordered. "And hide the copies in the cupboard."

Then they heard the big door of the massive building opening. Footsteps echoed through the halls.

"They are coming upstairs," whispered Cătălin. "What shall we do?"

"Quick, let's hide under the tables at the back," said Aunt Luci. "Don't breathe a word."

It was now dark inside the laboratory, and Carmen and Cătălin were praying, *Jesus, help us!* Soon they heard men's voices in the hall. They were walking slowly up the corridor, checking the handles of the doors. When the heavy footsteps arrived at their door, Carmen and Cătălin started to tremble. But soon the steps went away. After what seemed hours, they heard the big door at the main entrance again, opening and closing.

"Are they gone?" Carmen whispered. "I will go and see. Yes, they are leaving in the car."

Aunt Ani and Aunt Luci looked shaken as they came back to their working positions. The second session of typing and copying went slower. Cătălin thought he could hear steps in the hall all the time, and Carmen thought that every car passing by was a police car. They were praying all the time, *Jesus, help us!*

By eleven o'clock the copying was finished.

"Get all the copies together and let's go. We should leave everything in perfect order. Nobody should suspect that we were here," said Aunt Ani. "We will go out the back door."

Soon they were out of there, stepping as quietly as they could along the corridor and down the stairs to the back entrance. Aunt Luci opened it as gently as she could, and the door shut quietly behind them.

"The work is not finished yet," Aunt Ani said. "I would like to get the copies bound for you. I know someone who can do it. What is the name of your children's choir?"

"Sion," Carmen and Cătălin answered, and said good night to their aunts....

Another Sunday afternoon at the church, I was waiting for the children to come for choir practice. The door opened, and in came Carmen and Cătălin with two large shopping bags full of songbooks.

"Quickly, quickly," I said, "let's put them on each chair. And don't ever breathe a word about it."

When the children came, a big surprise was waiting for them. Each songbook was bound with a hard cover that had "Sion Children's Choir" in gold letters on the front. The children in the choir were amazed. It was the first songbook they had ever had. And despite a certain twinkle in Carmen's and Cătălin's eyes, nobody seemed to know where they had come from.

Chapter Seventeen

Christmas at Home

Viorel was a small boy of twelve who used to attend the children's choir during vacations. He had dark blue eyes, long curly eyelashes, and brown hair. He was dressed in his school uniform: a navy blue suit, black shoes, and a white shirt with a red scarf around the neck. That red scarf said, "I am a communist. I don't believe in God." But Viorel did believe.

Although Viorel was a boy, he could easily cry. Some boys laughed at him, but his mother said he had love in his heart. After all, wouldn't you cry in his place? He was at a boarding school in Reşiţa, miles away from his hometown of Iaşi. He missed his family, and especially the children's choir in the church. But that was the only school in the country that had accepted him to learn a craft. He was training to make musical instruments: violins, mandolins and flutes.

His best friend at school was Florin, a tall, skinny orphan boy with big brown eyes. His blue uniform seemed so large on him.

One day he asked Viorel, "Do you have a home?"

"Yes, of course," Viorel answered. "My father is a baker and we have a nice home."

"I wish I had a home. I've never once left this boarding school."

"Don't you have anyone?"

"No. Nobody has ever come to see me. It happens to other boys, but not to me. At times I feel so lonely."

"Soon it's the Christmas vacation. I'll see if I can take you home with me," Viorel said with tears in his eyes.

Florin looked at him with a ray of hope.

A few days passed, and Viorel could not take his mind from Florin. Finally he went to the headmaster.

"Comrade Mania, can Florin come home with me for Christmas?" Viorel asked.

"Impossible," said the tall, strong man with a moustache and metal teeth. "He is one of President Ceauşescu's children. He wants all the orphans for his secret army. You will have to ask permission from him!"

With his cap in his hands, Viorel bowed and made a quick exit. The headmaster might have thought he was finished with him, but he was wrong.

He went to the dormitory leader and made the same request.

"Foolish thought," the leader said. "Don't bother me. He is the property of the Communist Party."

Suddenly Viorel remembered how his older brother would get away with anything with the help of a doctor. So he knocked at her office. The school doctor was a young lady with short hair and glasses.

"Please," Viorel asked her with tears in his eyes, "can you give Florin a note that he needs to see a specialist? I want to take him home for Christmas. You see, my city has the best medical school in the country."

"Well," the doctor said, "Florin is indeed a sick boy. He has terminal cirrhosis of the liver. I could arrange the visit, but it's very complicated."

Viorel remembered how at the children's choir they prayed for everything and the Lord Jesus answered. Quietly in his heart he started to pray.

Then he heard the doctor talking on the phone. His heart beat fast as she talked back and forth with many people. One moment he was full of hope, and the next moment he thought it was all in vain. Then she spoke with his mother. After a while, a secretary appeared and typed all sorts of papers, which all had to be stamped and signed. It took ages.

"He can take Florin and go," he heard.

Viorel couldn't believe his ears.

He rushed into the dormitory to share the good news with Florin.

Soon the two of them were on the train to Iaşi.

When they arrived home, Viorel's family received Florin warmly.

They showed him around the house, and he gazed for a long time at the Christmas tree in the corner.

"It's so nice to be in a home!" Florin said as they took their seats around the table with the smell of freshly baked bread and cakes.

Every orphan in the world should have a friend like Viorel. Maybe you will be one of them. Jesus said: "I tell you the truth, whatever you did for one of the least of these brothers of mine, you did for me" (Matthew 25:40).

Florin was going to need his friend even more in the days to come.

Chapter Eighteen

The Baptismal Service

Jesus said: "Whoever believes and is baptized will be saved" (Mark 16:16). In Romania, baptisms were strictly controlled by the secret police. Candidates were intimidated, threatened, and sometimes refused baptismal permits. That is why the services were performed in secret in the forests at night, wherever there was water. My father performed such services, and I remember him coming home at dawn with his clothes wet.

One Sunday at church, during the children's choir practice, Viorel approached me. "Please come with me to the hospital. My classmate is there. He is an orphan, and he is dying. I wish so much that he would go to heaven."

I agreed and went with him the next day.

Parhon Hospital was a massive gray building on Copou Hill. It had a large garden with walkways and benches surrounded by a high stone wall with security guards at the gates. There, on the third floor in Ward Six, Florin lay on a white bed. He was a skinny thirteen-year-old, with big brown eyes and a very yellow face. His head was shaved.

"Don't be sad," I told Florin, taking him by the hand. "You have a Father in heaven. He loves you so much that He gave His only Son to die for you. He has a wonderful home for you in heaven."

Florin nodded and suddenly seemed so happy.

I visited Florin together with Viorel several times after that. One day he accepted Jesus Christ as his Savior. I gave him a New Testament.

"I love reading God's Word," he said.

"I love it too," Viorel answered. "But be careful."

"Yes, I hide it each time I hear steps in the hall," Florin answered.

Florin grew in the Lord very fast. Children from the choir visited him, and he even learned to sing a few songs. One day he read in the Bible, "Whoever believes and is baptized will be saved."

"I would love to be baptized," Florin said, "but how?"

"If you really desire that," I said, holding his hands in mine, "it has to be in secret. The authorities would never issue such a permit for you."

"I have an idea," Viorel whispered. "Let's baptize him in my parents' flat, in the bathtub. My aunt was baptized there, too."

"Yes, I can talk with one of the elders," I said.

The day of the baptism came. That evening nobody recognized the tall young man in a black suit and big hat as he left the hospital.

In Viorel's bathroom everything was prepared: a white gown for Florin, warm water, towels, and flowers. Luca, one of the elders, and Dan, the youth leader, were waiting there. They had had the courage to perform such baptisms before. The most solemn moment came when the elders asked Florin, "Do you believe that Jesus is the Son of God, and that He died for you?"

"Yes!" Florin answered, kneeling in the water, his hands clasped for prayer.

"In the presence of seen and unseen witnesses, I baptize you in the name of the Father, the Son, and the Holy Spirit."

Florin disappeared under the water for a few seconds while we were singing quietly, "Whoever believes is baptized."

I looked at Viorel. He had a big smile on his face, and so did Florin when he came out of the water.

Then we took Florin back to the hospital the same way we had brought him out. In two minutes Florin had changed from his black suit back into the hospital pajamas, and was lying still in his bed. Nobody ever discovered what he had done.

The doctors prolonged Florin's life, but could not do much else for him. One morning in May, when the tulips were in bloom, he died. But Viorel was content. He had done all he could for his orphan friend, and now he was sure that they would meet again in heaven.

Chapter Nineteen

The Temptation

N ear the railway line, in the Nicolina district of Iași, was a small house surrounded by flowers and apple trees. This was home for my cousin Cornelia, whom I had chosen to be the soloist of the children's choir. She lived there with her parents, two sisters, and a brother. Their house was poor, with mud floors, and had a kitchen with a wood-burning stove in the middle, on which they cooked their food. But Cornelia liked it there. She especially liked the whistles of the trains passing by and the crowing of the roosters in her yard.

She was fourteen, with light brown, long, curly hair. She had big blue eyes, a few freckles, and dimples in her cheeks when she smiled. She also had a beautiful voice, which she had given to God since she was seven. The children's choir was proud of her, and she was known in many churches in Romania. But her beautiful voice stirred the jealousy of the television station and local Communist Party.

One day Cornelia was called into the conference room at school. Three men and two women sat behind a long table, covered with a red tablecloth. They stood up and shook hands with her.

"I am the president of the television station," said a fat man dressed in a smart suit. "Take a seat. We heard that you have a marvelous voice, as soft as velvet and as strong as a waterfall. We came to make you a proposal. How would you like to sing on national television?"

"Oh! That sounds wonderful!" Cornelia's face beamed.

"You will be paid each time you perform," a lady next to him added.

"And you will be seen and heard on prime time every Sunday. What do you think about that?"

"We will take you everywhere by taxi," another man said with a wink. "It will mean, of course, that you will have to quit singing for God in the Baptist Church."

"What will I sing?" Cornelia asked anxiously.

"You will sing folk songs," replied the television man.

"That sounds exciting," Cornelia replied, biting her lip.

"If you cooperate," said the president of the Pioneers organization, "you might have the chance to go abroad and take part in international competitions." She was a woman dressed like Cornelia herself, in a Pioneer uniform: a white blouse, pleated blue skirt, and red scarf with the communist insignia.

"I would love to go abroad," Cornelia said.

"Now you have to give us an answer in one week," added the television president. "Is that all right?"

"Yes, of course."

That day the teachers treated Cornelia kindly, which they never had done before.

"Hi, Cornelia," the math teacher greeted her. "How are you?"

"Fine, thank you," she said, blushing. *He doesn't usually notice me.*

"Cornelia, I want to invite you out for a cake," the Pioneers president of her class said one day, when she met her in the hall.

"Thank you!" *What's going on? This is the first time she has spoken to me!*

Cornelia went home from school thoughtful that day.

"What shall I do?" she asked her mother.

"Well, we would be proud to see you on television," her mother said. "They really must want you."

"But who will sing as the soloist in the children's choir?" Cornelia wondered.

"Your sister, Miceta, has quite a good voice too," said her father. "Maybe she can take your place."

That night Cornelia could not sleep. *What shall I do? What will the children say if I leave the choir? They prayed for me for years. And Teodor took so much time to train my voice. What about Genovieva, who wrote special parts for me to sing?*

The next Sunday she went to the choir practice early. She had to speak to me.

"I'm so glad you came early," I said when I saw her. "I wanted to talk to you. Listen, you know my oldest brother, Dionisie. He has just visited me…secretly. He is an English teacher." I lowered my voice. "He had to sign papers that he would never have anything to do with the church. That was the only way he could get a job as a teacher.… Anyway, he told me that he took part in a regional conference, with teachers from all over Moldavia. Hundreds attended. Listen…this is private. Nobody else should know. The president of the Communist Party talked at length about our children's choir."

"Our choir! Why?" Cornelia asked in amazement.

"They even played a tape with us singing 'My Harp will Play for You' and 'The Good Shepherd,' with you singing as the soloist, of course."

"And?" Cornelia asked with great curiosity.

"Well, then the president started to rebuke all the teachers because none of their schools could make such a beautiful choir. He also said, 'The children's choir at the church sings better than the television children's choir, and that is unacceptable.'"

"That's wonderful." Cornelia laughed. "What else did they say?"

"I hope nobody hears me," I went on in a low voice. "The president said that the teachers should come and spy on our choir practices, see what this Genovieva does with the children, and do the same. Does she give them candies? How does she attract them? You see, they don't know anything about the Spirit of God! He also said that he would try to steal *you* from the choir. So, be very careful. And don't forget that you gave your voice to God when you were seven."

"Oh, Genovieva…that's why I came early," Cornelia said. "I want you and the children to pray for me. They called me in and proposed that I sing on television. I felt tempted, especially by trips abroad, which they offered me. That is the dream of my life."

Some other children arrived, and I quickly made known Cornelia's need for prayer.

"Do you remember when we went to Bucharest on a trip?" asked Mirela, the girl next to Cornelia. "We sang in churches. We were put up in the Baptist Seminary and Mrs. Bărbătei received us very well. She cooked a meal for all forty of us with her own money. I remember how she gave you a special treat, a box of chocolates."

"Yes, I remember," Cornelia replied, thoughtful. "We all slept on mattresses in a big hall and we had a good pillow fight. It was so nice. On that trip, it was my birthday, and the church on Strada Popa Rusu gave me a doll that was almost as big as I was. I still have that doll in my room. It was the only doll I ever had in my life." At this her eyes filled with tears.

Other memories suddenly flooded her mind. *When I was seven, I gave my voice to God and promised to sing for Him alone. I renewed my promise many times in prayer in front of the children's choir. How could I forget that?*

A few more days passed. The time came again for her to be called to the conference room. She sat down in the same chair, nervous, but sure of her decision.

"Hi, Cornelia!" They were all smiles as they greeted her.

"Well, what is our little soloist's decision?" asked the television man.

"Well…when I was a little girl, I gave my voice to God. I cannot take it back. I want to sing in the children's choir."

Five shocked faces stared at her from around the table. Their smiles disappeared. But Cornelia knew that God was smiling down at her. And that was all that mattered, whatever the consequences of her decision.

Chapter Twenty

Easter under Persecution

They trusted in him and defied the king's command and were willing to give up their lives rather than serve or worship any god except their own God" (Daniel 3:28).

Dorel was twelve. He attended the children's choir I was leading at the church in Iaşi. He had received the Lord Jesus in his heart and loved to read Bible stories.

It was the spring of 1978. General School Number 23 in the district of Copou was a two-story brick building. There was a large slogan across the front of it: "Glory to the Communist Party! Glory to its most beloved Son!"

In one of the classrooms were the fifth graders. Dorel was sitting at his bench with his hands behind his back, listening attentively to the teacher. He had short brown hair and a round face with rosy cheeks, and was dressed in his blue school uniform with a red tie, the symbol of communism.

"As you know, Easter is approaching," said Comrade Ionescu. "I would remind you that you are not allowed to attend church during this season." She had cold, blue eyes and blond hair. She had been the commander of the Pioneers for many years in that school, and all the children were afraid of her.

"I also want to remind you that it is forbidden to say, 'Christ is risen!' and 'He is risen indeed!' Anyone caught saying it will be punished or arrested. And one more thing: On Easter Sunday morning I want you all to come to school nicely dressed in Pioneer uniforms. We will meet here and walk in columns to the Statue of the Communist Heroes. We will sing songs of glory to the president. The band will be there to play and we will bow down when the drums beat."

Now Dorel had a difficult decision to make all by himself. His father was not a committed believer yet; his mother was a communist who did not even believe in God. In fact, she hated Christians.

On the way home Dorel remembered how he had become a Pioneer when he was eight. All the children were taken to a mausoleum. It was a spring day just before Easter. Soldiers played in a band. It was very solemn. Then each child had to recite aloud a vow and salute with his right hand. When his turn came Dorel said, "I, Dorel Târcan, swear that I will be a good communist. I swear that I will fight religion and mysticism with all my strength." Then Comrade Ionescu put a red tie around his neck. He remembered that after that he became very sad. He hated the memory of that day.

Two years later he made another vow. I led him in a prayer: "I, Dorel Târcan, believe that Jesus is the Son of God, and that He died for me on the cross and rose from the dead. I accept Him into my life as my Lord and Savior." He remembered that after that he became very happy. He loved the memory of that day.

As Dorel passed by his neighbors' houses he smelled *cozonac* from their brick ovens outside in the yards. It was a delicious Easter cake made with Turkish delight and flavored with vanilla.

His parents' small, white house had a well with flowers at the front and cows and chickens at the back. When Dorel arrived home his mother was there.

"Mom," he said while eating his soup. "Please let me go to church on Easter Sunday."

"Dorel," his mother answered, "I don't want you involved with those people. Besides, the authorities are very watchful at Easter time. They will catch you." She was short and plump with green eyes and straight hair.

"Mom, I am a Christian. I received Jesus Christ into my heart. I want to go to church."

"But Dorel," his mother said with her hands on her hips, "I don't believe in God, and I don't want you to believe either. So stop that nonsense!"

When Easter came, Dorel had to make up his mind.

Should I go to church or to school on Easter Sunday? If I go to school, everything will be fine. If I go to church, my mother will beat me up…and Comrade Ionescu will too.

When he went to bed that evening he asked the Lord for help. Then he remembered the story in the Bible about the three boys who refused to worship a statue and who were thrown into a fiery furnace. He too had to be ready to suffer.

Early in the morning when the rooster started to crow, he got up. He got dressed in his best clothes and sneaked out of the house while his parents were still asleep.

When he arrived at the church, the hall was packed and he joined the other children in the choir at the front. The preacher said from the pulpit, "Christ is risen!" And the congregation responded: "He is risen indeed!" Then there were many beautiful songs about how Jesus came to save people from their sins and about how He died and rose again. Dorel was so happy to be there.

A few days passed, and Dorel came to the church where I was living to speak to me. His eyes were downcast, his shoulders bent forward. As I held his hands, I saw bruises from beatings his mother had given him.

"Be very careful, Genovieva," he said. "My mother beat me up, and she wants to beat you up too. She was called to the secret police and had a long talk with Colonel Ceucă. He told her to throw stones at you and even kill you. She is very angry and I am afraid of what she might do."

"We will pray," I assured him, holding his hands to try to encourage him.

Several days later I went out with my brother Costică to run an errand in town. At a corner a woman suddenly shouted and threw stones at me. I covered my head with my hands, but I was too late—some stones hit me. It was Dorel's mother, Aurica. She swore and picked up more stones. Costică rushed toward her, trying to stop her, and I ran away.

Together with the children in the choir, we all prayed for Aurica. God answered our prayers in a most unexpected way.

Aurica started to have pain in her legs. When she went to the doctor she was told, "It is a blood infection. You have a gangrenous leg, and the infection will spread very quickly. We have to amputate from above the knee."

After a few months, as she lay in bed dying, she said to Dorel, "Please forgive me. Ask Genovieva to forgive me too. I want to become a Christian. I know that my life is almost over, and I am sorry I will never be able to go to church with you."

"I forgive you, Mom," said Dorel. "I am so glad that you now believe in Jesus."

"I also want to rededicate my life to the Lord," his father said.

Dorel was sad that his mother was dying, but happy that she now had eternal life.

It was worthwhile choosing to take a stand for the Lord, he thought. *My mother will not beat me up any more now...but what about my teachers?*

Chapter Twenty-one

The Last Wagon

It was spring again in Iaşi. Blue and yellow crocuses bloomed in the front garden of the church on Strada Sărărie. Inside the one-room building, kneeling with their heads bowed, fifty children were praying, "Lord, please help us to get to Caransebeş to sing for You there. Amen."

"Be very careful, Genovieva," my father told me after the children had gone home. He had been the elder in charge of the church in Iaşi since the pastor was murdered three years before. "They called me to the secret police and asked me to stop the choir from going," he whispered.

It was a time of great persecution for Christians. The country was under the cruel dictatorship of Nicolae Ceauşescu. But the persecution of believers was sophisticated, subtle, and well organized. The communists did not like to create public scandals, which would create sympathy for Christians.

According to the regulations, children were supposed to clean parks on Sunday mornings, not sing in church. Teachers would disguise themselves as monks and nuns and attend the Easter services, to see if any of their pupils was attending.

Women could not bake the traditional Easter cake, as the communists made sure that the ingredients could not be obtained. Two months before Easter they removed the flour, yeast, and vanilla or lemon essence from the shops.

In spite of opposition, I had traveled with the choir all over the country singing. The Lord had done many miracles on our behalf. *Will He help us again?* I wondered. *We have to have faith in Him, but also the readiness to suffer.* During the spring vacation we had been invited to go and sing in churches in another part of the country. We had spent many hours rehearsing Easter songs.

"What answer did you give the secret police?" I asked my father.

"'The Bible says that we must obey God rather than men,' I told them. 'Jesus said, "Let the children come to me and do not hinder them." My duty is to call children to God,' I said. 'It is your job, not mine, to hinder them.'"

"And?"

"'If *you* won't stop them, *we* will!' Commander Ionescu shouted at me. 'But you will pay for it!' He threatened me worse than ever."

"We've already bought the tickets," I said. "And everyone is excited about going."

"Give the tickets to the children," my father advised, "and tell them to come two by two. There is a law that forbids Christians from traveling as a group. So don't let them accuse you of that."

"Thank you, Father," I said, giving him a hug.

I remembered the evening when two elders came to talk to me in the back of the church. They had traveled all night by train from Caransebeş.

"Genovieva, please come with the choir to our area," said Rădoi, one of the elders. "The children in our churches need to learn from your choir to stand for the Lord."

"I heard," said Cocârţău, the other elder, "that wherever the Sion Choir travels, children's choirs spring up like flowers. That's exactly what we need in our county. Churches are waiting for you in Reşiţa, Oţelu Roşu, Obreja, Simeria, and of course Caransebeş."

"We will come the Friday before Easter if all goes well," I promised. "But we will really have to pray."

After a lot of practice, the children's choir was ready for the trip. They knew the twenty Easter songs by heart. Teodor, my brother, played the organ. Silvia, Nelu, and Costică played guitars. Poems and Scripture passages were to be recited between songs. Everything was well prepared. Finally the time came for departure.

On Good Friday at five o'clock in the morning while it was still dark, sleepy children arrived at the railway station from all directions. They carried little suitcases or bags in their hands. As they arrived on the platform they pretended they did not know each other and got on different carriages.

Soon the train left and, crowding at the windows, the children waved good-bye to their parents.

As the train picked up speed, we all regrouped in one carriage.

"Children," I said, trying to be heard by everyone, "be very attentive to my triangle on this trip. Each time you hear it ring, pay attention! It might just be a call for prayer, or...who knows what?"

"Yes!" they all answered.

"In Bucharest we change trains," I continued. "Don't get lost. Keep in twos all the time. We must look for the train to Caransebeş. Now we'll have a time of prayer. Let's all call upon the Lord for help. We have enemies who don't want us to get there."

After fifteen minutes of quiet prayer, the children started to play and tell stories. A few hours later they opened their lunch bags. The smell of hamburgers with garlic and fresh oven-baked bread was very inviting. The boys and girls soon forgot all about danger. But my heart was heavy.

"There are a number of secret police officers traveling with us in the first class compartments," said Teodor. "I wonder what they are up to."

"I was wondering too," I said. "Several times they passed by and counted us. 'Fifty-five,' I heard one of them say."

By eleven the train arrived in Bucharest. The children got off and followed me discreetly two by two. The Gara de Nord railway station was very busy as the children made their way to the platform for Caransebeş. The train was already there, and almost all of the carriages were full to capacity. The last carriage, though, seemed quite empty.

"Is this carriage going to Caransebeş?" I asked the tall man in railway uniform who was standing by.

"Yes, ma'am. Don't you see the sign?"

But why is it so empty? I wondered.

"Is this carriage going to Caransebeş?" Teodor asked another man, who had a whistle in his hand.

"Yes, sir, get on," he said.

The children followed Teodor and me into the carriage. Loudspeakers were announcing the train's imminent departure. *Why are the two men smiling at each other?* I thought as I watched them through the window. *What is he doing there? Changing the sign?*

I got off the train.

"There is something going on," murmured Teodor, jumping off too.

"Look," I said, "the Caransebeş sign on our carriage has disappeared. It now says Videle."

So they want to dump us in Videle, a dead end just outside Bucharest! Lord, save us!

There was no time to argue with the guards, so I quickly rang the triangle. All the children appeared at the windows to see what was happening.

"Get off!" I shouted at the top of my voice. "This carriage will be disconnected in Videle."

"Get on one of the front carriages," Teodor shouted. "Quick! We only have five minutes."

The children got off carrying their little cases, and ran to find empty spots in the overcrowded carriages.

"No room in this carriage," a woman's voice shouted.

"Please, make room for me! I have to get on," little Claudia pleaded.

I stood on the platform with Teodor, Silvia, Nelu, and Costică until each of the children had gotten on one of the nineteen front carriages. *Are all the children on?* I wondered. *Lord, help them!* As the train began to pull out of the station, we also jumped on.

After five hours of traveling, the crowded train arrived in Caransebeş. I jumped off and ran along the platform from carriage to carriage ringing the triangle loudly. Teodor counted the children as they got off. "Forty-six...forty-eight...fifty! Praise the Lord! All the children are here!"

About ten cars were waiting to transport the children to the church.

"We have been threatened by the secret police," Rădoi told me. "They said they would beat us up and confiscate our driver's licenses if we transported the children. We are ready to pay the price though."

"One of the elders had a vision," Cocârţău shared. "He saw angels all around the choir, protecting it. That encouraged us all."

When we finally arrived at the church, we found the building overcrowded, with many worshipers standing outside. Children welcomed us with flowers. There was an introductory prayer and a word of greeting. Then the children started their program. The Sion Choir sang wonderfully that night, and many people had tears in their eyes.

But what will happen to the children when they get home? I wondered.

Chapter Twenty-two

The Parade

Y ou shall have no other gods before me. You shall not make for your-self an idol in the form of anything in heaven above or on the earth beneath or in the waters below. You shall not bow down to them or worship them" (Exodus 20:3–5).

It was a Sunday evening in the spring of 1978. The church service was over. As usual I had led the children's choir that evening. We had about forty-five minutes in the program. Several hundred people had listened to the children's singing and then to the sermon that the guest pastor had delivered. Now everyone was ready to go home, and I hugged the children in the choir one by one as they left. When I came to Mirela, a girl of twelve, she started to cry.

"Why do you cry?" I asked, taking her hand. "Please tell me."

"Because every Sunday evening when my sister and I return home from church, our mother beats us up."

Mirela was a slim girl with green eyes. She had a quiet, pleasant spirit, and it saddened me to learn how much she suffered because she was in our choir.

"She is a communist and says that there is no God in heaven," her sis-ter Daniela added. "She says that the Communist Party is god." Daniela was ten, with dark hair and brown eyes. She was full of life and very talk-ative, but now she too had tears in her eyes. "We are afraid to go home."

"You have both been so faithful to the Lord ever since you gave your lives to Him three years ago," I said, hugging them. "You never missed a

Sunday. Regardless of the weather, rain or snow, you were here to serve the Lord. You, Mirela, recite so well. And you, Daniela, are such a good soloist for the choir. The Lord is proud of you, and He will certainly protect you and help you to remain faithful to Him."

By now several other children had seen them crying and joined me in prayer for them.

Mirela and Daniela left the church and took a bus home. By nine o'clock they arrived at their apartment. They lived in the Nicolina district near the Bahlui River, in one of the dozens of blocks of flats. The elevator took them to the third floor. They tiptoed to the door of their apartment and Mirela put the key in the lock as quietly as she could. *Lord, help us!* they prayed.

When they got inside all was silent. Their parents were sound asleep. Their three-room apartment was decorated with Persian carpets on the walls and floors and dark oak furniture. They went into the kitchen, each grabbed a piece of freshly baked cinnamon bread, and went straight to their bedroom.

"Thank You, Lord," Mirela whispered as she pulled her cover over her. Daniela smiled for joy and fell asleep.

On Monday morning their parents went to work and the two sisters went to school. The school was two blocks away from home. It was a large three-floor brick building with many classrooms and a sports field. Usually the teachers were very severe and gave them a lot of work. But today was just before the May 1 holiday. That day and August 23 were days when all working people, students, and children were forced to worship the president with songs and dancing, bowing down to him or his portrait. Schools and factories alike stopped all activities early every day for two weeks, in order to practice for the parade. Mirela hated those days. She knew that God forbade worship of anything or anyone but Himself.

Her teacher explained, "We will dismiss classes early. We will go to Copou Hill and from there walk to the center of town. Be very attentive. This is the final practice. Everything has to be perfect. The military band will play. The television and high officials will be there, perhaps even the president. We will approach the stage stepping in the rhythm of the music. Then we will stop and turn around to face the stage and the portrait of the president. When the music stops and the drums beat, each of you is to run to your own place and bow down on your knees, with your head touching the ground. The president will see that we write with our bodies words of praise to him, 'Glory to our president.' On May 1, at six o'clock in the morning, you all have to be at Copou Hill dressed in your parade uniforms. The roll will be called and attendance is compulsory."

When May 1 came, early in the morning Mirela and Daniela's mother woke them up at five o'clock.

"Eat your breakfast and get ready," she said. "It looks like wonderful weather for the parade."

Then the girls' parents left for their factory to join their group for the festivities.

Mirela and Daniela got dressed in their yellow and blue dresses and went to their meeting point on Copou Hill. All over the town the streets were already crowded with thousands of people going to their meeting points to wait for their turn to worship the president. Many were holding flags on their shoulders with the president's name on them. Others were holding balloons and flowers. The smell of popcorn and grilled sausages filled the air. Over the next six or seven hours everyone had to be ready to bow down to the god of communism.

There were slogans all over the town that read, "Praise to Ceauşescu, Prince of Peace," "Glory to the Son of Man, Nicolae Ceauşescu," or "Praise and Honor to our President and to the Communist Party, Bringer of Happiness."

Mirela knew that such words belonged only to Jesus, and had been stolen by the communists and given to that evil dictator.

"I wish we would never have this parade," she told her sister on the way to their meeting point.

"Me too," agreed Daniela. "Maybe it will rain."

"Yes, let's pray that it rains and that it is canceled. I don't want to bow down to anyone but Jesus Christ," Mirela agreed and they exchanged a smile.

Then Mirela became thoughtful. *Lord, I wish I could run away from this parade. I feel so lonely. The teachers are spying on me and my parents too. The only joy I have is to go to church and praise You with the children's choir.*

Soon they arrived at Copou Hill and waited there for two hours until the parade was to start. It was a bright, sunny morning with a clear sky. By this time all the streets were barricaded by police and soldiers, and no one could escape and go home.

By eight o'clock Mirela and Daniela were already tired of standing up and waiting. But God was watching over them. Suddenly they felt a breeze and saw that the sky had become cloudy. After a few minutes they felt the first raindrops. Soon it was pouring rain.

The barricades were lifted, and the May parade for that year was officially canceled. Everyone was told to go home. Mirela smiled. Deep down in her heart she felt that God loved her very much and believed that He sent the rain just for her.

The children's choir continued to pray for Mirela and Daniela, especially that God would touch their mother's heart. However in the next weeks things got worse at home.

One evening the girls finished their homework and were ready to go to bed. They put the lights off, knelt down at the side of the bed, and prayed. Then Mirela heard a noise outside the bedroom door. *Has someone been listening to our prayers?* she wondered.

Suddenly the door flew open and their mother shouted, "To whom are you praying? There is no God up there. I forbid you to pray!"

"Mom, He is there and He hears us." Mirela knew her bold words would anger her mother, but she needed to speak them anyway. "And Jesus is in our hearts."

Slapping them in the face, their mother swore at Jesus.

"Mom," Daniela pleaded, "don't swear at Jesus. I love Him so much! He is so good! If you swear at Him one more time I will cry until I die."

"It would be better to have you dead than Christians," she screamed.

Furiously she took hold of Daniela and Mirela's hair with both hands. She pulled them to the right and left, then knocked their heads together. The girls cried out in pain.

"From now on I will lock you in every Sunday. Never again will you go to church!"

To Mirela, it was the end of the world. And she couldn't stop Daniela's crying. But God, whom they loved so much, was watching and He had other plans.

The next day, their mother felt very sick. Being a member of the

Communist Party, she had access to the best doctors. They did tests on her then said, "It looks very bad." Immediately they called her husband and told him his wife had an incurable disease. She had less than a year to live.

Lying in bed with high fever and pain, the mother called her daughters.

"You have been such lovely girls, and I mistreated you. Please forgive me. Tell me about Jesus, about God. I want to become a Christian too."

Mirela and Daniela explained to her all they knew. That Jesus died for our sins on the cross and His blood cleanses us from all our sins. They also taught her John 3:16: "For God so loved the world that he gave his one and only Son, that whoever believes in him shall not perish but have eternal life."

"Yes, I believe," she said.

And Jesus filled her heart with peace and joy. Their father also turned to the Lord.

In the spring she died. Mirela and Daniela, though sad, were so thankful to God that their mother was saved. They knew that they would meet her again in heaven.

The communists knew that the girls' mother had become a believer through their testimony. What would the consequences be?

Chapter Twenty-three

Hidden Microphones

H ow many boxes of Bibles did you receive?" Mr. Negru asked my
nephew Iulian.

Iulian was sitting in the interrogation room at school. He was a small twelve-year-old, nice looking, with brown eyes and brown, curly hair. He accompanied the children's choir on his guitar.

"What Bibles?"

"Don't pretend that you don't know," Mr. Negru shouted. He was a young secret policeman, tall with wavy, blond hair and dark glasses. "You counted them and told your sister, 'There are fifty in each box.' Remember?"

Iulian was silent.

"We have our ways of finding out everything. Now get out of here!"

Iulian went home somber that day. He and his sister, Corina, had lived with my family since they were small.

How do they know what we talked about? Iulian thought. *Lord, help me!* He was worn out, having spent four hours in the interrogation room. The same man had tried to persuade him to give up the children's choir not long before. In the same room, one of his teachers had beaten him over his fingers until they were bruised and swollen.

He had been involved in receiving Bibles since he was eight. His job was to make sure that the street was clear. He would walk up and down, observing everything that was happening. When the road was safe, the Bibles were brought and unloaded quickly.

"Corina, they heard what we said in the living room," Iulian whispered to his sister and grandmother when he got home. "I don't know if it's safe for the next load to be delivered here."

"How do they know?" Corina asked. She was one year older than her brother and had light brown hair tied up in a ponytail.

"I don't like our neighbors," Iulian said. He had a bad feeling about them.

"Neither do I," Corina agreed. "All sorts of strange men come and go."

Iulian thought that over, and the next day he had an idea. He came home from school at two o'clock. *I really must have a talk with Ionel. His parents get back from work at six.*

He put a piece of pink bubble gum into his mouth and went out, pretending to play.

"What have you got there, Iulian?" asked Ionel, his seven-year-old neighbor.

"Don't you see? A red double-decker bus." Iulian showed him the toy, and then he put another piece of gum into his mouth.

"Where did you get that? I have never seen one of those before," said Ionel, looking with fascination at the bus.

"It's from friends of my aunt in England. You can play a little with it if you like."

"Can I have some bubble gum? I always wanted some, but my mom says there is none in the stores."

"I'll give you a whole packet on one condition," said Iulian.

"What?"

"Show me your toys in your room."

"Come with me," Ionel agreed.

Iulian followed Ionel into the house adjoining theirs. Ionel's parents were Communist Party members and had good jobs.

"Nice house you have," Iulian said as they stepped onto the Persian carpet in the living room. There his eyes went up and down, right and left, taking in everything.

"What is that?" Iulian asked, pointing to a reel-to-reel recorder.

"That's a tape recorder," said Ionel. "You press the button and it records what you say. Some men came and put it there. My father puts it on when you have guests. Then the men come and take the tape."

That was all Iulian needed to see.

"Thank you, Ionel. You can keep the bus as well as the bubble gum."

So that's how they heard me counting the Bibles! Shall we cancel the next shipment? he wondered. *Lord, help me to know what to do.*

Once Iulian was back inside his house, he told Corina and his grandmother about his discovery. From that time on they talked only in whispers when it concerned anything secret. *Are the other rooms bugged as well?* Iulian wondered. He went around the house, searching for anything suspicious.

Then a few days later he thought he heard something beeping. They had no radio in the house, and no electronic equipment.

"Corina," he called his sister, "do you hear that?"

"Yes! Where could it be coming from?" she whispered.

They followed the sound. It took them to the chimney.

"It must be a microphone," whispered Grandma. "When your grandfather was alive he found one in the attic. They start beeping when they go wrong."

Iulian got down on his knees and looked up the chimney from the fireplace.

"I have to go on the roof," he whispered.

Grandma walked around outside to keep watch, while Corina kept the ladder.

"Lord, help me," Iulian said as he climbed up to the chimney. "There it is," he said, grabbing a wire attached to the chimney pot and pulling it up. There was a metal object as small as a walnut on the end. It was making a beeping sound.

"Look," he whispered when they were back in the house.

"What shall we do with it?" whispered Corina.

"Let's bury it at the back of the garden," said Iulian, while Grandma was putting the ladder away.

They quickly made a hole in the ground, and put the beeping microphone in it. Then they covered it with earth and stepped on it until no more sound could be heard.

"It's dead," said Iulian, and they laughed.

Another week passed, and the next load of Bibles was safely delivered.

But the secret police knew that something was wrong.

Mr. Negru interrogated Iulian again at school. "What did you do with the microphone?"

"What microphone? I don't know what you are talking about."

The secret police continued to plant microphones, but Iulian had made it a little more difficult for them to listen to our family's conversations.

Chapter Twenty-four

The Hiding Place

That evening the Sion Children's Choir sang in front of a crowded congregation. One of their songs was inspired by Psalm 91: "You will not fear the terror of night.... If you make the Most High your dwelling...then no harm will befall you." The children sang this song beautifully. *But are they going to remember those words when trouble comes?* I wondered.

Iulian and Corina and their cousins, Babi and Laura, were going to be put to the test that very night after they arrived home from church. Their grandmother, with whom they lived, had gone away for a few days to visit relatives in another town.

"Keep an eye on the cellar," she had told them before she left.

"We will," Iulian had assured her.

He was now fourteen and had a pleasant face with dark, intelligent eyes. He had a sense of humor, and dimples in his cheeks when he laughed.

Corina had a pretty face, white teeth, and thoughtful brown eyes. She was wearing the white blouse and long skirt she usually wore for church.

When the church service was over, the four of them took a tram up Copou Hill and got off at the stop for Strada Coşbuc. Then there was a ten-minute walk to their home. It was dark but they were not afraid, at least not yet.

When they passed the bend in the road, they could see the house. Suddenly Iulian noticed something suspicious.

"The lights in the kitchen are on," he said, and they all stopped. "I'm sure I checked everything before we left. Someone must be in the house."

"Let's go back to the church," Laura suggested. She was nine, with long straight hair. She wore her best green corduroy dress. Her big eyes looked scared.

"The gate is wide open. We locked it when we left," said Babi, a blue-eyed boy of eight with blond hair. "Let's hide in the park!"

"We can't leave the house empty any longer," Iulian replied. "I promised Grandma that I would keep an eye on the cellar...."

The cellar was located in the yard, close to the rear of the house. People thought that it was a just a storage place for vegetables. But in reality it was a hiding place for thousands of Bibles. To get into it you had to open a door and go down seven steps. Inside were shelves with potatoes, cabbages, and parsnips. Behind the shelves, a double wall led into a secret tunnel where the Bibles were hidden.

Iulian remembered that his grandfather had taught him, "Whenever you are in danger, call upon the Lord. He will help you."

"Let's pray," Iulian said.

"Lord, give us courage and protect us!" they all prayed.

The children couldn't go to any of the neighbors for help. Everyone avoided them because of their Christian faith.

Fearfully, the four children entered the yard. All around the property was a wire fence with an iron gate, which the family kept locked. There was a rose garden at the front and a large flowering bush which spread its branches to the ground. At the back of the house was a large vegetable garden, some apple trees, vines, and a woodshed.

The small white house had an entrance hall, two bedrooms, a kitchen, and a pantry. When they entered the house, their hearts beat fast.

"Somebody has moved my bed around," said Laura, and her eyes darted around in fear. "They might be hiding under it."

"The wardrobe too. Look, the clothes are in a mess!" Corina added.

It happened once before, Iulian remembered, *when I was very small. Grandpa said that the secret police liked to search houses without a warrant, looking for Bibles. That's why they came like thieves, while we were out.*

After looking under every bed, in every wardrobe, and in every corner, the children were convinced that there was no one hiding in the house. Then they were able to relax.

What about the hiding place? Iulian went quickly to check. He stepped down into the cellar with a flashlight. *Yes, everything is in place.*

He came out carrying a bag full of potatoes. He didn't know, but those potatoes would be very useful that night.

"Now, let's forget about our troubles with a piece of apple pie," Corina said. "I helped Grandma bake it before she left." Corina also boiled some milk and gave each of them a cup.

Before going to bed, Iulian read Psalm 91 to them aloud. He had to encourage everyone, especially Babi and Laura, who were their guests. The Lord reminded them again through His Word: "You will not fear the terror of night.... If you make the Most High your dwelling...then no harm will befall you." They locked the gate and the door and put the lights off. Then they prayed and went to bed. Soon they were all sleeping peacefully, but not for long....

The telephone rang.

Iulian picked it up. "Hello!"

"This is Colonel Ceucă," said a low voice. "May I speak with Mrs. Sfatcu?"

"She is not at home," Iulian answered, rubbing his eyes. He looked at the clock on the wall. It was one o'clock.

"Then I shall speak with you. We heard that you are hiding Bibles. Where are they?"

Iulian's grandfather had taught him to answer questions in such a way as to confuse the enemy. "Bibles? I don't understand. What are you talking about?"

"We will come and see. If we find any, you will all end up in prison." *Click.*

The children were all awake by now. They were praying on their knees. "Lord, protect us and don't let them find the Bibles!"

After fifteen minutes they heard a car pull up outside.

The children stood in the dark with the lights off. They saw two men get out. One was big and tall, and the other was short. They both wore dark clothes. They were carrying some strange-looking sticks.

"They have flashlights too," said Babi.

"It must be Colonel Ceucă and Major Mekenie," Corina whispered.

The two men opened the gate with a master key and went straight to the far back corner of the yard. They started to tap the ground inch by inch with their sticks.

"What are they doing?" Laura asked.

"They are checking for underground tunnels," Corina explained.

Soon they will be near the hiding place, Iulian thought. *Lord, what shall we do?*

Then Iulian remembered something his grandfather had said. The secret police hated public scandals and noise. They liked to operate in the dark when no one could see them. He suddenly knew what to do.

"Babi, come with me," he whispered. "I need your help. We have to wake up all the dogs in the neighborhood. They will help us."

Through a small window, the two boys quietly crawled outside. Iulian took the bag of potatoes with him. They hid in the flowering bush and started to throw well-aimed potatoes onto the roofs of the houses in the street.

Boof-boof! Boof-boof! was heard on every rooftop.

Almost every home had a dog, and they reacted immediately.

Woof-woof! Woof-woof!

Then the boys crawled back into the house.

Now the neighbors were emerging in their pajamas, complaining to each other about unusual thuds in the night.

The secret policemen didn't have any time to waste. They had to be out of there before the dogs got after them. They got into their car and disappeared into the night.

After half an hour all was quiet again in the street. The children fell asleep in peace, and the Bibles were safe.

God always helps us when we trust in Him and serve Him with courage, and so the children too were safe for now.

Chapter Twenty-five

The Forbidden Book

M y niece Corina was a faithful member of the children's choir. She was also involved in underground work with Bibles. One day she was getting ready to leave for school when the telephone rang. She rushed to answer it.

"Hello!"

"Corina, this is Adriana. Can you bring me the book you promised?"

"I'll do my best."

"See you then." And she hung up.

I hope they didn't understand that conversation, Corina thought. Many of their calls were recorded.

She went straight to the back of the garden. They kept vegetables there in the underground cellar for the winter. She lifted the cover and went down the seven steps. Behind the heap of potatoes was the secret opening where Bibles were hidden. She took one, hid it under her sweater, grabbed a few potatoes in her hands, and came back out into the garden, replacing the cover after her. Then she went to her room to get ready for school. *Will they catch me?* she wondered.

Her grandfather used to say, "The Bible is a book to be highly treasured and shared with all." He was dead now, but his words were still alive in Corina's heart.

"I would so much like to have a Bible," Adriana, her classmate, had told her the week before. "My grandmother was a believer and she owned one. Before she died she told me stories about Jesus Christ, how He loved us and died for us. When she died my parents hid it away out of fear. It was a very, very old book."

"Then I will bring you one sometime, but don't ever say I gave it to you."

"I would like to have a faith like yours," Adriana said. "If I read the Bible, maybe it will help me. You are so peaceful and kind."

At one o'clock, Corina and Iulian left for school, a twenty-minute walk from their home. They both wore the dark navy uniforms with a red tie around their necks. This tie was supposed to remind them that they had taken an oath to be good communists, not to believe in God, and to fight religion. Children who refused to take this oath were taken away from their parents and put in communist orphanages.

The school was housed in a massive two-floor building for over one thousand pupils. The pupils had classes in rotation, some of them going in the morning and some in the afternoon. Corina and Iulian attended the afternoon session.

"Be careful," Iulian told his sister as they were approaching the school. "You know Brother Ursan who attends our church? He went to buy bread the other day in a store. While waiting in line, he accidentally got his Bible out of his bag. He intended to put the bread at the bottom and the Bible on the top. A policeman saw him and arrested him. 'Don't you know it's forbidden to show your Bible in public?' he shouted."

"That's terrible," Corina replied. "I heard that if they see you giving a Bible to someone, you can be put in prison for religious propaganda. But our grandfather always seemed to find a way around these laws. I mean to as well."

Corina's first class was Marxism. The thirty-six pupils became quiet when Mrs. Frost, the Marxism teacher, entered. She was small, with short hair, green bulging eyes, and large nostrils. She wore high heels and an elegant red suit. She went straight to her desk, but instead of starting the class she made an announcement.

"I have received orders to conduct a search today," she said in a severe tone. "Schoolbags on your desks, and hands behind your backs!"

Corina's heart pounded and she prayed, *Lord, help me!*

One after another, Mrs. Frost looked through each pupil's belongings.

She found horoscopes, playing cards, forbidden magazines, and cigarettes, but didn't say a word.

Lord, help me! Corina prayed when Mrs. Frost arrived at her desk. Her schoolbag was emptied upside down on her desk. Corina turned pale, seeing the Bible fall out in full view of the teacher.

"What is this book?" asked Mrs. Frost.

"It's a Bible," Corina answered.

"Did you bring it to school?"

Silence.

"Answer me!"

The whole class was staring at Corina.

If I say I brought it for Adriana I will get her into trouble, she thought. She pressed her lips shut tight.

"I will call the police," said Mrs. Frost.

Soon a policeman arrived, wearing knee-high boots and armed with a rubber stick in his hand. The headmistress came too, and a photographer who took pictures of Corina with the Bible on her desk.

They want to put me on trial, she thought. *That's why they take pictures.*

"Those who believe in this book are very dangerous," said the policeman, holding up the Bible.

"Besides this, we were informed that Corina taught children to pray," added Mrs. Frost.

"Why did you bring this book to school, Corina?" the policeman asked.

"It's my Bible. I love it. I do not go one day without reading it."

The policeman seemed puzzled, and the children listened in silence.

"Don't you know it is forbidden?" the policeman asked, and he smacked Corina's bench with his stick.

"This book gives me hope and peace."

"Shut up!" he shouted. "If you keep on talking like that I will put you in a correction home."

"From now on," the headmistress announced, "Corina will sit in the last bench. I want empty benches to the right and left and in front of her. Treat her as if she had a contagious disease," she said to the other pupils. "From now on treat her as deaf and dumb."

Then Corina was taken into an empty room and left there for several hours. She was hungry and felt like she might faint. Iulian was brought in too. A secret policeman hiding behind dark glasses came to interrogate them.

"If you don't give up going to the church and playing guitar with the children's choir, we will put you both in a state orphanage."

He hit them with a stick until they both started to cry.

"Where did you get the Bible?"

"Our grandfather left us one," Iulian answered.

"Do you hide Bibles at home?"

"In our house?" Corina asked. "No."

"We will have to search your house."

Soon two secret policemen took Corina and Iulian home and searched every room and cupboard in the house. They even ripped open a mattress. They also went into the attic.

"What do you have in that cellar?" one of them asked as they were leaving.

"Cabbage and potatoes," Grandmother answered.

Lord, blind their eyes, Corina prayed.

The man with dark glasses went down a few steps.

We are finished, Corina thought.

But then the man turned round in disgust.

"It's muddy down there!"

Thank You, Lord, Corina prayed when the two men left.

Corina went back to school the next day, even though she thought that all was lost. *Nobody will want a Bible anymore after what happened.*

But she was in for a surprise. Adriana, her classmate, whispered to her when no one was looking, "Corina, you did great. You had so much courage! And your face was shining. You were so calm! All the children were admiring you, I could see that."

"Do you still want a Bible?" Corina asked her.

"Yes," Adriana answered, "and several other girls would like one too."

When she arrived home, Corina remembered how her grandfather used to leave Bibles hidden in different places, and then tell people where to go to get them. This way, if the person receiving it was caught he could say he found it.

Less danger on both sides, Corina thought.

Several days later when they met at school, Adriana smiled happily. Corina knew why and she smiled back. She was more than ever convinced that the Bible was a book to be treasured and shared. This belief kept her going, even though the president of Romania would target her family in his war against the Bible.

Chapter Twenty-six

The Message

B e strong and courageous. Do not be terrified; do not be discouraged, for the LORD your God will be with you wherever you go" (Joshua 1:9).

President Ceaușescu was leading a war against the Bible. My family was at the top of the wanted list because of their underground work. "Get the Sfatcus," he ordered. "They should all be put in chains."

Iulian was a Sfatcu and he wondered, *Will they arrest me too?*

There was tension in town, and fear seized the whole church. Many had hidden away their Bibles. Even the word *Bibles* sent fear into people's hearts. Police were everywhere, searching homes for Christian literature and preventing people from gathering for evening prayer. Telephone lines were cut, the mail was stopped, and communication between believers was almost impossible. There were arrests, beatings, and interrogations.

Iulian, though only fifteen, was in the middle of it. Two of his uncles and their wives were under arrest. Six hundred Bibles had been confiscated from their hands. Iulian knew a lot about the underground work.

"You should never say a word about it," they taught him. And he never did.

He was a small boy for his age, but he looked so mature. His beautiful curly brown hair, deep brown eyes, and slightly pointed nose made him look like a musician. He was, but there was no time to play the flute or guitar now. He'd inherited humor from his grandfather, and that, together with his courage, often got him out of trouble. He remembered how his grandfather used to say, "The Lord is always with you, so be strong."

Today, his grandmother, who had raised him and his sister, Corina, took him aside and whispered in his ear, "Go to Rădăuți, to Uncle Avram. He has to have this message." She handed him a cassette.

Iulian put the cassette under his shirt, grabbed some money from a drawer, and set off. He walked fast on Strada Coșbuc, his hands in his pockets, kicking little stones on his way, trying to pretend he was relaxed. Inside, though, he was painfully alert. *Help me, Lord! Help me, Lord!* he repeated in his heart.

Since the time he was eight he used to be sent out to walk this distance, almost a mile, with the order, "Go and see what's going on." He would go and observe everything: cars waiting for no reason, men with dark glasses hiding behind telegraph poles, curtains moving strangely at windows with watching shadows behind them. He would bring back the most accurate report. If it was safe, the Bibles were brought in a van and unloaded in the dark in their underground cellar. From there they were distributed with much care.

Help me, Lord, to get the message to our contacts, Iulian prayed. *If they don't get this cassette, they will make the wrong move.* He did not look back at all. But his ears were very attentive. He heard steady footsteps behind him. They sounded like the boots of a soldier. *Am I being followed?* He quickened his step to catch a tram that was just pulling in. The steps behind him hurried too. He bought a ticket at the back door of the tram then he made his way through the crowd toward the front door of the wagon, ready to jump out if necessary.

I have to deliver it or destroy it, he thought. The tram was heading toward the center of town, close to the train station. Iulian looked through the window and saw many girls and boys his age laughing and playing happily. How different his life was from theirs!

In a few minutes the tram was there. Iulian jumped off and ran toward the station. He heard the same boots running behind him. He ran faster, and the boots ran faster too. Now he was sure he was being followed. There was no time to waste. He dashed into the station restroom, locked himself inside, took the cassette from under his shirt, threw it on the floor and crushed it under his heels. Then he flushed everything down the toilet.

Taking a quick look to make sure that no trace was left, he came out. It had taken him less than a minute.

"So there you are," said the man, puffing and panting, as he arrived. Iulian looked for the first time into the face of his pursuer. He was a heavy man in his fifties, with a revolver at his side. "Why did you run like that?" the man demanded, his rough hands thoroughly searching Iulian's body.

But he didn't find anything and Iulian returned home.

"I couldn't do it," he told his grandmother with tears in his eyes.

"At least it did not fall into their hands," she said. "Maybe God will give us another chance."

That same evening Iulian tried again with another copy of the message. This time he took his sister, Corina, with him. They took a suitcase full of clothes, hiding the cassette in the middle.

"Let's go," Iulian said. With their grandmother's silent prayer over them, they left. It was pitch dark. Corina was a year older than Iulian, and she'd had many adventures because of her faith. It was raining now and the wind whipped the leaves and branches. When they arrived at the wooded area of the street, someone appeared from behind a tree.

"Stop! Don't move."

A strong light shone into their eyes and on their suitcase. It was a policeman.

"What have you got in there?" he asked, pointing to the suitcase.

A moment of silence followed. Iulian thought everything was lost. His heart pounded. Suddenly he knew there was only one thing to try.

"Bibles!" he replied and started to laugh.

Corina joined him.

"Are you joking with me?" the policeman shouted, and then he started to curse. "Get out of my sight, crazy kids."

And that is exactly what they did. At midnight they arrived at their destination and delivered the message. The work with Bibles was protected—at least this time.

Chapter Twenty-seven

A Kernel of Wheat

In Romania talking to someone about Jesus was forbidden. The Bible was an illegal book. Many Christians lived in fear and some died in mysterious circumstances....

Gabi was seventeen. She had long black hair, and her slanted brown eyes gave her a pretty, exotic look. She was one of the first members of the Sion Children's Choir, which I started in my church in Iaşi. She lived with her parents and two younger brothers in an apartment building by the River Bahlui. From her room on the third floor she could almost touch the branches of the fir trees that surrounded the block.

Gabi played the guitar and wrote several songs about Jesus. She carried on her shoulder a handmade cotton bag, in which she had her big Bible. It was full of markings and notes and underlined all over. When she arrived for choir practice on Sunday afternoons, the children would shout, "Gabi has come! Gabi has come!"

March 4, 1977, Gabi and her friends were praying in her apartment at sunset. The sky was a copper color. Suddenly the building started to shake.

"Earthquake! Out!" Gabi's mother shouted.

Gabi, her family, and her friends rushed down the stairs as fast as they could. They joined the hundreds of people who were already outside, running away from the buildings in fear. The blocks of apartments were shaking like wheat in the wind.

But suddenly Gabi ran back toward the block.

"My Bible! My Bible!" she exclaimed.

"Gabi! Gabi!" her mother shouted.

"Come back!" screamed Ella. But Gabi disappeared into the building.…

In a few minutes she was out again, gasping and holding tight her Bible.

"I can't live without it! I can't live without it!" she said while the earth was still trembling.

Everyone admired Gabi for that, except for the secret police.…

Gabi often came to share her troubles with me at the church. "My father joined the Communist Party, and my mother drinks," she told me one day. "I feel so lonely at home. My only joy is to come to the children's choir and to read my Bible."

One day the secret police summoned her for interrogation at their headquarters in Copou. She prayed all the way to the large, gray, three-story building on Strada Codrescu.

A guard opened the heavy door and escorted her to room 307. It was a room on the ground floor with a high ceiling and barred windows. On the wall was a picture of President Ceauşescu. In a soft armchair sat Major Mekenie, a dark-skinned, middle-aged man of Turkish origin. He was smartly dressed in military uniform. He motioned to her to take a seat on the hard bench in front of him.

"Miss Gabriela, we heard that you are in possession of a Bible. Where did you get it?"

"I…I found it under a bench," Gabi answered.

Her pale face blushed, and her heart beat fast. *Lord, help me!* she prayed.

"You Christians always seem to find Bibles under benches. Why don't I ever find one?" he asked as he lit a cigarette. "Do you know who put it there?"

"I don't know," she said.

Then he started to pace the floor, showing the red stripes on his shoulders and the blue decorations on his chest.

"Who comes to your home on Saturday evenings?" asked Mekenie.

"My friends."

Don't you know that it is illegal to meet in homes? Give me their names."

Gabi put her head down. *I will never give any names. I will not be an informer.*

"We know everything!" he said. "Tatiana, Mihaela, Liliana, Mariana, Daniela, and Miceta. You call yourselves The Seven, don't you?"

"Yes." Gabriela nodded.

"There is a new girl who came last week. What is her name?"

Gabi looked down. Her lips trembled. *I will never tell you. You will not touch Silvia.*

"We heard that your group prays for Israel. I warn you that if you don't stop such meetings, you will be killed. Are you also involved in illegal Bible distribution? Look this way!"

Gabi looked at him, then looked down again. *You can do anything to me, but you won't make me talk.*

"One more thing," the major added. "You invited your bench-mate, Silvia, to join the children's choir at the church. I warn you, leave her alone! Now, get out of here."

Gabi went home. That week at school, all forty pupils in her class had to fill out a questionnaire. It had questions like "Do you believe in God?" "Do you pray to him?" "Do you have a Bible?" "Do you attend religious meetings?"

Gabi answered yes to each question. But then she wondered, *Where will the questionnaire go? To the secret police?*

After classes that day, Gabi talked to Silvia. Silvia was a small, blond girl with blue eyes.

"How did you answer the questionnaire?" Gabi asked.

"I…I answered no to all the questions," she replied. "I was so afraid!"

"When you give your life to Jesus, He is with you and helps you not to be afraid."

"You know, I liked going to church with you. I especially liked singing in the children's choir. But it is too risky for me to come with you anymore." Silvia would not look at her. "The teacher warned me to keep away from you."

"Do as you please," said Gabi, trying not to feel hurt. "But remember that I will always love you and pray for you."

Later that year Gabi started nursing school. Her classmate there was Iolanda, the daughter of a secret policeman.

One day Gabi's class was taught how to give injections.

"Would you allow me to practice on your arm?" Iolanda asked.

"Go ahead," Gabi answered and presented her left arm.

But why are her eyes so restless? Gabi wondered. *Why does she tremble like that?*

Soon Gabi became sick and had to give up her studies. Her left arm swelled up to double its normal size. For about a year she was confined to bed. Finally, the doctors had to amputate her arm.

"Gabi is dying," her mother told me, wiping her eyes.

"She was such a good child," her father added.

The elders of the church came to give her communion. The children in the choir took turns to visit her and they cried.

"Don't be sad. I will go to heaven," she said. "What a joy it will be to see Jesus!"

One day she asked her friend Mariana, "Please read me Psalm 17:15."

Mariana opened the Bible and read aloud: "And I—in righteousness I will see your face; when I awake, I shall be satisfied with seeing your likeness."

When she finished reading, Gabi closed her eyes and went to be with the Lord.

Several weeks passed after Gabi's funeral. The children's choir was practicing at the church for the evening service. Gabi's chair remained vacant. No one wanted to sit on it. The children missed her and only wanted to sing songs about heaven.

Suddenly the door opened. The children looked and saw a blond girl with blue eyes come in. It was Silvia, Gabi's former bench-mate. She walked slowly to the front.

"I came to share something with you all," she said and burst into tears.

It became quiet and the children listened to her.

"I had a dream," Silvia said. "I dreamed that I died and went to hell. It was a dark place with ugly faces everywhere. There was a lake of fire and the smell of sulfur. I was terrified and screamed for help. Then, suddenly, in the distance appeared Gabi. She was beautiful, with a long white dress and a golden crown on her head. She looked straight at me and smiled."

Silvia paused.

"I want to go where Gabi is," she cried. "I don't want to go to hell! Please, accept me back into the children's choir."

The children clapped their hands for joy as Silvia took her place on Gabi's chair.

I closed the choir practice that afternoon with the words of Jesus: "Unless a kernel of wheat falls to the ground and dies, it remains only a single seed. But if it dies, it produces many seeds" (John 12:24).

We held tight to these moments of joy; the secret police were everywhere and any of us could be arrested at any moment.

Chapter Twenty-eight

Petru's Mission

I n 1979 in the city of Iaşi, finding a secret place for the Easter service was important, especially when the speaker was a foreigner.

"Please help me to find a safe place," I asked Petru, a boy in my children's choir, as we sat on a bench at the back of the church one evening. He was a boy of twelve, of medium height, with green eyes and freckles. He liked to dress in his yellow check shirt and light blue trousers.

"I'll try my best," he promised. "The secret police should not know. They trouble my grandfather all the time and interrogate him about Bibles."

Petru knew that every year teachers disguised themselves as monks or nuns and attended Easter services. They came into churches, knelt down, and pretended to pray…but in reality they spied on children. When they saw one of their pupils there, they immediately called the police.

"A service held in secret is much safer," I said.

Petru took his job very seriously. He walked for hours through the forests. *If we are caught, it will be my fault*, he thought.

Finally, he chose a place near a monastery at the top of a hill. It was a meadow of green grass, nestled in the forest, where the wild cherry trees were in blossom. To reach it you had to take a steep footpath for a mile up the hill. The next day he passed the word around.

Easter morning arrived. It was sunny weather on Cetăţuia Hill. The mauve and pink lilac bushes spread their fragrance.

At half past eight, thirty boys and girls from the children's choir arrived.

"Christ is risen!" they said as they arrived and joined the group.

"He is risen indeed!" the others replied. They sat in a circle on the soft grass. But Petru was on duty. He walked up and down, observing everything.

My friends Silvia, Dǎnuţ, and Vieru tuned their guitars and started to play. Everyone sang an Easter song and the birds joined in: *Cheep-cheep!*

> He is alive! He is alive!
> My Lord is risen!
> He is forever alive!
> And to those who believe in Him,
> He gives eternal life and happiness.

Bzzz-bzzz! Bees accompanied the young people as they sang many songs that morning.

Then it was the turn of our speaker, the Danish missionary, Ulf. He was hated by the secret police, but much loved by the Christians. He read from the Bible and shared the story of the resurrection. He said, "The Son of God died and gave His life for us. God raised Him from the dead.... If we believe in Him, God will also raise us from the dead...."

The hours passed quickly. Soon lunchtime came.

Petru's grandparents and Aunt Silvia brought the food. They had prepared it at home, because they lived at the bottom of the hill. They set the food on the grass on a tablecloth. Ulf thanked the Lord for the meal of stuffed cabbage, sheep cheese, olives, salami, and homemade bread. Vieru brought cold water in a wooden bucket from a nearby well. We finished the meal with freshly baked *cozonac*, the traditional Easter sweet bread with its aroma of vanilla. Everyone ate with thanksgiving.

After we ate, I told Ulf, "It will be wonderful to spend the whole afternoon with you here. The young people have many questions from the Bible."

"I would be glad to," said Ulf.

Little did I know....

Petru's mission was not finished. He saw a monk watching them from one of the monastery windows. He didn't like the sly look in the man's eyes. *Is he really a monk?*

The elders brought bread and wine and served communion.

During that time, Petru climbed to the top of a locust tree and looked around in all directions. He could not believe what he saw…. Five or six police cars surrounded the hill. They parked at the bottom. The police got out and started to climb the hill with fierce police dogs that strained at their leashes.

In a second he climbed down the tree and jumped to the ground from the last branch.

"Police," he shouted. "They have surrounded the hill!"

"We have to run," I said.

"They have dogs and will let them loose on us!"

"On our knees!" Ulf shouted. "'May God arise, may his enemies be scattered; may his foes flee before him!'" (Psalm 68:1).

The whole group repeated that verse aloud after Ulf.

How will the Lord save us? I wondered.

Suddenly, the wind started to blow. Clouds filled the sky and darkness cloaked the hill. I felt a few raindrops on my face. Then the rain poured down in a violent storm. The blossoms blew in the wind like swirling snow.

"Now we can run," said Petru. "The dogs cannot smell us in the rain. See you at my grandparents' house!"

Everyone ran through the undergrowth. They grasped hold of bushes and trees and slipped and slid down the hill. In fifteen minutes, everyone was at the bottom. I was wet through, muddy, and full of scratches.

Petru had been the first to arrive at the bottom. He guided us one by one to the back door of the house.

"We are all free!" he said, gasping for breath.

"Hallelujah!" everyone shouted.

After a while the rain stopped. Petru peeped through the back window.

"Look, a rainbow!" he said.

Then he saw the policemen and their dogs get into their cars and leave. They were soaked to the skin and looked exhausted.

There was no doubt in my mind. *The Lord of Easter is risen and is with us! But are we ready for what might come next?*

Chapter Twenty-nine

The Feet of a Deer

One year during the summer vacation I was invited to take the children's choir to sing in churches in the north of the country. After a train journey of four hours we arrived at our destination. We admired the mountains covered in green forests under a deep blue sky. Flocks of sheep and goats grazed beside the streams. The houses were painted mauve, blue, pink, and green like Easter eggs. The villagers went about their work in national costumes embroidered with silver and golden thread. The wooden fences were painted with pictures of roses. It seemed so peaceful that one might have thought that there were no secret police around to persecute Christians. But we were soon to find out otherwise.

The family that hosted the fifty children and five adults served us a meal under the shade of a huge oak tree in their yard. The children loved the sheep cheese and apple pie.

"There is no time to waste," I said to the children after the meal. "Let's go and practice for the evening service in the forest at the foot of the mountain. Many will come to hear you sing. We need to be well prepared."

Within half an hour we were all sitting on a soft carpet of thick grass in a forest clearing. Little blue and pink flowers showed their beauty all around us and nearby the children found wild raspberries.

Teodor, Silvia, and Nelu tuned their guitars, and I chose the first song. It was beautiful to sing praises to God together with the whole creation. Bears, foxes, and deer lived not far away.

"Can we sing 'There is a flag?'" asked nine-year-old Gabi.

"Of course we can," I answered, "and we'll do the actions that go with it."

Soon all the children were singing as loudly as they could, accompanied by guitars and by the birds in the trees.

> There is a flag flying high
> From the castle of my heart,
> From the castle of my heart,
> From the castle of my heart.
> There is a flag flying high
> From the castle of my heart,
> For the King is in residence here.
>
> So let it fly in the sky,
> Let the whole world know,
> Let the whole world know,
> Let the whole world know.
> So let it fly in the sky,
> Let the whole world know
> That the King is in residence here.

We had hardly finished singing when we heard from behind, "Stop! What are you doing here?"

We all looked at the man standing there dressed in a dark blue uniform with shiny buttons and a peaked cap. He held a little walkie-talkie and was trying to communicate with the police station.

"Lord, save us," I started to pray.

I remembered how a friend of ours, brother Ulf, had once been in danger after distributing New Testaments in the street. His enemies chased him. He ran and ran, with several men pursuing him.

Suddenly he came to a high stone wall and thought that he would be caught. At that moment the Holy Spirit flashed into his mind a verse from the Bible, Psalm 18:29: "With my God I can scale a wall." The next thing he knew was that he had jumped over the wall, leaving his enemies dumbfounded.

There was silence now in the forest. The singing had stopped and the chirping of birds seemed to have stopped too. The children were scared and stared at the policeman.

"What are you doing here?" he repeated.

"We are playing…and singing," I answered.

"I heard you. You sing forbidden songs. And don't you know that Christian meetings in the forest are illegal? Now everyone follow me to the police station. Understood?"

I took Gabi and Cristina, two of the younger children, by the hand.

Lord, save us! To the police station? He will fine us and interrogate us. We will never get out of there in time for the evening program. The church and the children in the village will be so disappointed!

We followed the policeman in silence to the edge of the forest like lambs to the slaughter. When we reached the main road, the Holy Spirit brought to my mind a verse from the same psalm: "He makes my feet like the feet of a deer" (Psalm 18:33).

"Let's run!" I said to the children. In a moment we all overtook the policeman and ran ahead of him with the feet of a deer.

"I am losing them! I am losing them!" he mumbled into his walkie-talkie and ran after us as fast as he could.

"I will get a few of you," he said, gasping for breath. "Stop, little boy!"

But six-year-old Petronel shot off like a rocket.

"I will get you, little girl. Stop!" he shouted.

But little Laura flew like a bird.

After a few minutes of running I looked back and saw the policeman sitting down by the side of the road, puffing and panting.

"He has given up," I said. "Thank You, Lord!"

"Thank You, Lord!" the children responded.

That evening the choir sang many praises to the Lord, who had saved them once again from their enemies.

Chapter Thirty

The Wall of Protection

It was the summer of 1979. One evening, at the church where I lived in Iași, there was a knock at the door. It was one of the elders from the Baptist Church in Vicovu de Sus, Aurel Coroamă. He made a hand signal that let me know he wanted to speak to me in secret.

We went outside and sat on a bench.

"I come in the name of four churches in our area," he said. "We want the Sion Children's Choir to come and sing in our area for the glory of God. You traveled hundreds of miles all over Romania, but you never came to Vicovu. It is only three hours away from Iași. The children can also have a few days of vacation in the mountains."

"We will come," I said. "Shall we plan it for the first week of September, before school starts? This way I will have time to prepare the trip with my brother Teodor."

"That will be fine. You will all stay at my place. I have a large house. Don't forget that Christians are not allowed to travel as a group, but two is not considered a group."

"I will tell the children to come two by two from the railway station to your house," I said.

"Here is money for the train tickets," he said and handed me an envelope.

"Thank you."

I was delighted at the thought of making this trip with the choir. *But will the children be safe?*

The next Sunday, in the orchard behind the church, I gave the good news to the children.

"Keep quiet about the trip," I told them.

Over the next few weeks, Teodor bought the tickets. The trip by train to Vicovu went well. The children pretended they did not know each other, and no one noticed that we were a group.

Two by two the children walked from the train station to Coroamă's house. Long tables were set up in the garden behind the house. The ladies prepared chicken borscht with lovage, sheep cheese with corn mush, and homemade bread. Hay mattresses were spread all over the house, even in the attic.

For the first three evenings the choir sang in packed churches. There was no trouble with the police. I thought the last evening would be the same....

That afternoon the children were with me in the garden. The adults were there too. We had a rehearsal time for the evening program. We prayed on our knees that the Lord would use us for His glory.

"I would like us to repeat 'The Lord is my Shepherd' one more time," I said.

A beautiful harmony came from the choir and instruments.

> The Lord is my shepherd,
> I shall not be in want.
> He makes me lie down in green pastures,
> He leads me beside quiet waters,
> He restores my soul....
> Even though I walk
> Through the valley of the shadow of death,
> I will fear no evil....

Abruptly the singing stopped. The children spoke among themselves as they looked toward the gate at an unexpected visitor wearing a large hat. It was a secret policeman with an angry face.

"Stop!" he shouted.

The children all became quiet. From the gate, he looked over the whole group. Then he stared at me and pointed with his finger.

"You," he said. "Come to the police station with me."

"Me! Why?" I asked.

"You sing forbidden songs. Just come."

I quickly found my shoes in the grass and put them on. I tidied my hair and started to pray. My heart beat fast. I knew I was in trouble.

The policeman turned his back to us and waited for me. I had a minute to say good-bye to the children. *I might never see them again*, I thought. I hugged Ligia, Gabi, Cristina, and Petronel, the youngest ones. "Pray for me," I told them.

The children came around me: four, then five, then ten.… The circle became bigger and bigger and tighter and tighter. Soon they all crowded around me. I could not take a single step.

"Don't go. Don't go," the fifty children pleaded.

The smaller children started to cry.

"Don't go, Genovieva. Don't go!"

The policeman became impatient. "Are you coming or not?" he shouted.

I tried to go, but I could hardly breathe, pressed by the children.

"Sir, I can hardly move. You come and get me!"

He took a few steps toward me. At this point, all the neighbors in the street came out of their houses and watched. The policeman did not like that. He suddenly turned around and left.

"Thank You, Lord!" the children shouted.

Will he come back? I wondered. *Should we resume the rehearsal? The service starts in two hours.*

The children's tears had hardly dried when they heard the sound of a car approaching. It stopped near the gate. The same man got out, accompanied by another officer in uniform. The officer hid his eyes behind big dark glasses. In a second, the children formed the wall around me again.

"Miss Genovieva," the uniformed officer said politely. "We received orders to take you to the police station for a simple identity check. In half an hour we will bring you back to your children. Please come."

"Don't go, Genovieva!" the children said and started to cry again.

The officer was very upset. The cries of the children became louder and louder.

"Jesus, help us! Don't go, Genovieva!"

All fifty children were crying and praying in desperation. The voice of the policeman could no longer be heard. He made signs to me and ordered me to come.

"I have to go," I said to the children. "Let me pass. Make room for me." But it was a waste of time. The children did not move an inch.

"Do you hear? Come! We are waiting for you!" the policeman roared.

"Come and get me," I said. "I cannot move. I am stuck here!"

The two policemen stepped toward me. I imagined that they would scatter the children with their batons, but instead they turned around and left. I saw them get into the car and drive away.

The children calmed down.

"What a relief! Thank You, Lord!" they said.

Then Cornel and Iulian had an idea. "We will watch at the gate while you practice in the garden. If anyone comes, we will let you know."

I went back to the practice and resumed the same song:

> I will fear no evil,
> For you are with me.…
> You prepare a table before me
> In the presence of my enemies.

Half an hour passed, and I thought our troubles were over.

But suddenly Cornel and Iulian came running. "A car is coming! It is a jeep with three aerials."

The vehicle stopped outside the yard. I knew it came from the Securitate.

Quickly the wall of protection arose around me. Two new officers got out. They spoke from behind the fence with calm voices to win the children's trust.

"Miss Genovieva," one of them said. "We received a written order of arrest. The commander of the secret police in Suceava is waiting for you. You must come with us."

"I understand," I said and nodded.

I tried again to clear a way to the officers. But the wall of children prevented me. All fifty children were now crying and praying.

"Miss Genovieva, we cannot return to our commander without you," the other officer said.

"Come and get me," I told them. "I cannot get out!"

They took a few steps…but then it was as if an invisible power much stronger than their order turned them around. They left and didn't return that night.

Oh, how wonderfully the children sang that evening!

Chapter Thirty-one

When Children Pray

The Sion Children's Choir had a reputation for their wonderful singing. Everyone was in awe as they listened to the children praise the Lord. Wherever the choir sang, new choirs were born for the glory of God. The secret police hated the choir for that. They fined anyone who transported the children in cars and confiscated drivers' licenses.

It was the winter of 1979 and Christmas was approaching. We were in Oradea, about three hundred miles from Iaşi. In spite of the persecution, pastors had invited the children's choir to come and sing in their churches. The last stop on our tour was Tulca, a village about sixty miles from Oradea. Hundreds were waiting for us in the church there.

How will we get to Tulca? I wondered. *There is no public transportation to that village.*

The Lord had blessed us in Oradea on that trip. The children knew more than forty carols by heart. They also knew Scripture verses, which they recited between songs. The instrumentalists played beautifully. Thousands came to hear the children and to record their singing. The streets were full of people who could not get inside. At the largest church the crowds even produced a traffic jam. The children were rewarded with baskets of apples, oranges, nuts, and candy. They loved the fondant candy wrapped in red, yellow, blue, and green foil.

I desired very much that the Lord would bless us in Tulca as well. I talked with my brother.

"Tudorică, we have to find a way to get there."

"What about Magda?" he suggested. "She works with the Tourist Bureau. Her job is to organize buses and drivers for tourists. You know how much she loves the children's choir."

I called her.

"I will try my best," she said.

Soon there was good news for the children.

"All is arranged," she said. "Sixty children and five adults for December 25. Wait outside the train station at four o'clock. I have paid the driver to take you there and back. Don't breathe a word to the driver that you are Christians. Only Communist Party members are allowed to use these buses."

"I will tell the children," I said.

Christmas Day arrived and we waited at the train station.

"The driver should not know that we love Jesus," I told the children as we waited for the bus.

"We will be careful," ten-year-old Cristina answered. She held the emergency prayer triangle in her hand.

The bus came. The driver, a big, tall man, opened the doors. He got off and lit a cigarette. "Get on, kids!"

The sixty children got on and chose their seats. The other adults—Silvia, Elena, Teodor, and Dănuț—sat at the back with their instruments. I took a seat behind the driver, next to Cristina and her younger sister, Gabi.

"Wow! What luxury," twelve-year-old Daniel exclaimed.

The children settled in their soft velvet seats.

"It is nice and warm in the bus," said Corina, a girl of nine.

"Everyone aboard?" the driver asked.

"Yes," I said. "We are all here."

The driver closed the doors and started the engine. Soon we were out of town and drove through villages in the country. We saw shepherds as they led their flocks of sheep. Smoke rose from the chimneys of the houses. Then we did not see any more houses, but only white fields.

As the bus entered a forest, it began to snow.

Then a little boy, Petronel, started to hum his favorite song. The whole choir and the guitars joined in:

It is snowing outside
With big snowflakes;

Everywhere is beautiful:
The gardens have put on
Their whitest garments.
And as I watch the snowflakes
Floating gently in the air,
I am happy that through Jesus
I am as white as snow.

> *Like a snowflake,*
> *Like a snowflake,*
> *Through Him I want to be;*
> *A snow star,*
> *A little white star*
> *Shining for Him*
> *Day and night.*

I thought the driver was enjoying the song....

Abruptly, the bus stopped at the side of the road. The engine shut off. The driver stood up, red with anger. He opened the front doors.

"Are you Christians?" he asked me.

"Yes."

"Then get off my bus!"

The children listened, stunned.

"But sir.... we paid for the tickets like anyone else."

"You deceived me!"

"Sir, please take us to our destination."

"I do not transport Christians in my bus!"

"I am responsible for these children. You cannot leave us here in the middle of a forest. It is snowing outside and it is getting dark. There might be wolves."

"Everyone get off my bus!" he said and opened the rear doors too.

"Sir, please take us at least to the next village," I pleaded. "Don't push us off in the snow on Christmas night!"

"Off!" he said. "If you don't obey, I will drive you all to the police station!"

While I was pleading with the driver, Cristina struck the emergency prayer triangle: *Cling-cling!* The children close to the aisle knelt down.

The others bowed their heads. With their hands together and eyes closed, they prayed.

The driver looked at them.

"What? A bus full of praying children!" he exclaimed.

Then it seemed as if an angel came and fought with him. He became weak and started to tremble. His face turned pale and was all sweat. He moved his hands through his hair and wiped his face with a handkerchief.... Then he sat down at the wheel, closed the doors, and started the engine.

"I will take you wherever you want," he said. "And I'll bring you back too!"

"Thank you!" the children shouted and clapped their hands.

Soon we arrived in Tulca. The packed church waited for us. The candles from the Christmas tree spread their gentle light over the congregation. Gifts wrapped in cellophane and tied with ribbons lay under the tree for the choir. On the platform, the children started their program with the carol "For unto us a Child is Born."

The driver sat at the back and listened for two hours to our entire Christmas program. At the end, with tears in his eyes, he told the choir, "I've never heard children sing as beautifully as you!"

The Sion Children's Choir was under special protection from the Lord, and as hard as the secret police tried to destroy it, they never succeeded. Wherever the children traveled similar choirs were formed, using the same songs. The efforts of the secret police to imprison or kill me also failed because God did not allow me to fall into their hands.

Chapter Thirty-two

A Strange Invitation

O ne day in the autumn of 1979 I received a strange invitation. A high-ranking officer in the secret police came from Bucharest to see me. He wanted to talk with me privately.

"Take a seat," I said, as I received my guest in the front room of my family's house on George Coşbuc.

"I am Colonel Ştefănescu," the small man introduced himself. He took his hat off and made himself comfortable in an armchair. "Miss Genovieva," he said, smiling at me from behind his tinted glasses, "I was sent by the Ministry of Religious Affairs in Bucharest to apologize for all the trouble we have caused you in the last seven years. It was a great mistake."

"What trouble, Mr. Ştefănescu?" I asked from my chair in front of him.

"The authorities committed a great error in expelling you from university in 1972. We know how hard you tried to get back in, but we blocked your efforts, both in Iaşi and Bucharest."

As I looked at him in amazement, I was praying for wisdom from the Lord. The word *fox* came to my mind.

"Well, the high officials in the secret police in Bucharest invite you to go back to university, in whatever city you wish. All your exams will be considered valid, and we might even help you to go straight into the third year."

A year or so before, someone else had made a strange proposal to me. He asked me to translate a book into Romanian. It was a theological book of considerable length, and I was promised a good payment. Then a brother sent a message to me: "Don't accept the job. He did that to two other Christian workers to take them away from their work in the church and to occupy their time. Then he didn't pay them anything and destroyed the translations."

Are they again trying to take me away from the work with the children's choir? I wondered.

"If you really want to show me kindness," I said, "then speak to the Baptist Union in Bucharest and allow them to hire me as a cleaning lady, with a proper working card. Three times the elders sent my application to Bucharest and I was refused. I am a daily worker and still in danger of being arrested for being unemployed anytime I go in the street."

"We want to do much better than that," he said, still trying to win me over. "You are an intelligent girl and you deserve a good career. We don't want you to stoop to the position of cleaning woman anymore."

"I won't accept it, Mr. Ştefănescu. I am so happy serving my Lord and Savior in the church, even if I have to clean floors."

Then he tried to approach me on another level.

"I grew up in an orphanage," he said, "and was forced to serve in the secret police. If you don't accept my offer I will lose my job."

"I wish you knew Jesus as your Savior. He is so wonderful that losing a job for Him would be worth it."

"Please…accept our offer," he begged and knelt at my feet. "I have a wife and three children. They will remain without bread if you refuse me," he said and started to cry.

"I listen only to God, Mr. Ştefănescu. Let me be a cleaning woman at the church."

Then Mr. Ştefănescu stood up, and his tone became smug. "Then let me tell you that from now on you are not allowed to work at the church. Someone else was given your job. The elders of the church already know."

He left and I went back to the church. I knew he was serious. In the last year I hardly could go anywhere without being followed by two or three agents. They followed close behind me, like bodyguards. I was never alone, which made me very tired. Friends from the church saw that my life was in danger and decided to accompany me day and night. Rodica, Nora, and Mariana took turns staying with me. The secret police did not like to hurt someone when there were witnesses.

My father was not there anymore to support me with his wisdom and courage. The secret police had poisoned him and he had died. Three young seminary students were offered at different times the position of pastor in our church in Iaşi. Each one of them was taken aside by the secret police and told, "You can have the position on the condition that you expel Genovieva from the church." But they refused.

Now where could I go? I fell asleep crying and asking the Lord for His help.

That night I had a dream. I dreamed that an angel took me far away from my country, into a wheat field. There was wheat ready to be harvested all around me as far as I could see. Wheat grew all over my feet and even on my soles. I woke up so blessed by that dream, although I didn't understand its meaning.

During the last several years there had been publicity in the West about my persecution—in newspapers, on the radio, and in official documents for human rights. The secret police hated bad publicity, and the government wanted it to appear that there was freedom for Christians in Romania.

On February 24, 1980, I unexpectedly received a passport and was told to leave the country within twenty-seven days. I was told to go to the United States and never to return.

The commander of the secret police, Colonel Ionescu, called me to sign for the passport. That was the last time I would be in that dreadful building. Holding my passport in his hand, he took me by the arm and led me from door to door. He would knock and then say, "Say good-bye to Genovieva! She is leaving for America."

"The most expensive girl in Romania is leaving," Colonel Ceucă added with a smile. "Good luck to you! Go and make as many children's choirs in America as you want," he said, shaking my hand.

"Good-bye," said Mr. Mekenie, coming out of his office. He had interrogated me many times. "Go and write songs in America."

"Oh, Miss Genovieva, have a good trip," said Mr. Negru, another officer who had threatened me many times. "You can even print songbooks in America," he said, smiling coldly. "Here it is forbidden."

They didn't know that they were prophesying.

The American Consul in Bucharest had a file on my persecution in

Romania. President Jimmy Carter did all he could to rescue Christians whose lives were in danger behind the Iron Curtain. I was one of the cases they monitored. I was received in America with the best visa, that of a political refugee.

My dream came true. I spoke in many churches and sent many food parcels to my country. Also I wrote new songs about Jesus and had them secretly taken into Romania. Of course, I kept in close contact with the Sion Choir and I received many letters from the children. From America, I could do a hundred times more for them than I ever did in Romania. After the revolution in 1989, I was able to multiply my efforts. For more information, please visit our Web site: www.genovieva.org.

The children's choir continued to sing and even travel after I left the country. My brother Teodor took over as director, with my friend Silvia as his helper.

APPENDIX

The following stories from this book have appeared as articles published in Christian magazines:

"The Wall of Protection" [The Divine Touch, abridged] (*Guideposts*, New York, January 1997);

"The Forbidden Book" (*Purpose*, Mennonite Publishing House, Scottdale, Pennsylvania, April 13, 1997);

"When Children Pray" (*Sunday Digest*, Cook Publishing, Colorado, November 23, 1997);

"The Song Book" (*Bread for God's Children*, Bread Ministries, Arcadia, Florida, December 1997);

"When Children Pray" [Christmas under Persecution] (*Covenant Companion*, Covenant Publications, Illinois, December 1997);

"The Temptation" (*Touch*, GEMS, Grand Rapids, Michigan, April 1998);

"Petru's Mission" [Easter in Hiding] (*The Wesleyan Advocate*, The Wesleyan Church, Indiana, April 1998);

"The Christmas Guest" (*Bulletin de Nouvelles*, CSEM, Geneva, Switzerland, November–December 1998 and *Women Alive!*, Overland Park, Kansas, November–December 1998);

"When Children Pray" (*The Joyful Woman*, Joyful Christian Ministries, Tennessee, November–December 1998);

"When Songs are Forbidden" (*Power for Living*, Scripture Press, Colorado Springs, Colorado, November 15, 1998);

"When Children Pray" (*The Link and Visitor*, Baptist Women's Mission Society, Ontario, December 1998);

"The Last Wagon" (*The Church Advocate*, Churches of God Publications, Findlay, Ohio, December 1998);

"When Children Pray" (*Christian Renewal*, AKCC Foundation, New York, December 14, 1998 and *Junior Trails*, Gospel Publishing House, Springfield, Missouri, February 7, 1999);

"Petru's Mission" [Easter in Hiding] (*High Adventure*, Royal Rangers, Gospel Publishing House, Springfield, Missouri, March 1999);

"Hidden Microphones" (*God's World News*, God's World Publications, Asheville, North Carolina, March 12, 1999);

"The Forbidden Book" (*Straight*, Standard Publishing, Cincinnati, Ohio, July 25, 1999 and *The Vision*, United Pentecostal Church International, Hazelwood, Missouri, August 22, 1999);

"The Recording Session" (*Power Station*, Scripture Press, Colorado Springs, Colorado, November 21, 1999);

"Christmas at Home," (*High Adventure*, Royal Rangers, Gospel Publishing House, Springfield, Missouri, December 1999);

"Christmas under Persecution" (*The Minister's Family*, LifeWay Christian Resources of the Southern Baptist Convention, Nashville, Tennessee, December 1999 and *Christian Standard*, Standard Publishing, Cincinnati, Ohio, December 5, 1999);

"When Children Pray" [The Christmas Trip] (*The War Cry*, The Salvation Army, Virginia, December 11, 1999);

"When Songs are Forbidden" (*Gems of Truth*, Herald and Banner Press, Overland Park, Kansas, December 12, 1999);

"Christmas under Persecution" (*The Shantyman*, Christian Courier, St Catherine's, Ontario, Canada, December 13, 1999);

"Hidden Microphones" (*Living My Faith*, Regular Baptist Press, Schaumburg, Illinois, March 19, 2000);

"The Song Book" (*The Vision*, United Pentecostal Church International, Hazelwood, Missouri, March 19, 2000);

"The Hiding Place" [The Cellar] (*Live*, Gospel Publishing House, Springfield, Missouri, June 11, 2000);

"Hidden Microphones" [The Truth Smugglers] (*Guide*, Review and Herald Publishing Association, Hagerstown, Maryland, July 29, 2000);

"The Red Umbrella" (*Junior Companion*, Herald and Banner Press, Overland Park, Kansas, September 3, 2000);

"When Children Pray" (*Gems of Truth*, Herald and Banner Press, Kansas, December 23, 2001);

"A Price to Pay" [Searching for a Job] (*The Vision*, United Pentecostal Church International, Hazelwood, Missouri, July 14, 2002);

"The Last Wagon" [Guardian Angels] (*Teens on Target*, United Pentecostal Church International, Hazelwood, Missouri, May 18, 2003);

"When Songs are Forbidden" (*Gems of Truth*, Herald and Banner Press, Overland Park, Kansas, reprinted December 11, 2005).